GIRLS
Resist!

A Guide to **ACTIVISM**,
LEADERSHIP, and
STARTING A REVOLUTION

by KaeLyn Rich

QUIRK BOOKS
PHILADELPHIA

Library of Congress Cataloging in Publication Number: 2017961224

ISBN: 978-1-68369-059-7

Printed in China

Typeset in Active, Sabon, and Utopia

Designed by Andie Reid
Illustrations by Giulia Sagramola
Production management by John J. McGurk

Quirk Books
215 Church Street
Philadelphia, PA 19106
quirkbooks.com

10 9 8 7 6 5 4 3 2 1

For Remi Lee

MAY YOU ALWAYS
BE AS CONFIDENT
AND FEARLESS AS
YOU ARE TODAY

Contents

This book
is for
girls.

This book is for girls who have something to say, for girls who have something to get off their chests, for girls who are ready to use their voices to slash through injustice.

This book is for girls who want to live boldly, who have a red-hot fire deep down in their gut, who are smart enough to be mad and bold enough to demand change.

This book is for girls who have had enough of inequity, who believe in a world where all people are treated fairly, who care deeply about their own rights and the rights of others.

This book is for girls who are loud, who are quiet, who are shy, who are outgoing, who are book-smart, who are street-smart, who are funny, who are serious, and who are a little bit of all of the above.

I wrote this book for girls—for *you*—because I was once a girl, because I'm the parent of a girl, because I truly believe girls can change the world, and because girl activists *have* changed the world. The girl revolution began long ago and continues today.

Girls Resist! is a guidebook, a launching pad, if you're ready to start taking action right now. You'll find everything from starting a campaign and organizing an online petition to fundraising for a cause and talking to the press. You'll find stories of real girl activists who have altered the course of history or are doing so today. You'll find a roadmap to making change happen, whether you choose to start with your hometown, your school, your country, or the whole world.

Girls' activism matters because girls are often told they *don't* matter. But this harmful judgment is not always so visible as someone saying: *You don't matter.* It can be much more subtle and hidden.

Yes, girls are doing a lot better now compared to decades past. More than ever, girls are participating in every sport and excelling in STEAM fields (science, technology, engineering, arts, and mathematics), though girls are still way underrepresented compared to boys. More young women than men are enrolling in medical and law schools and graduating from college. So why do I think that girls are told they don't matter?

Because I remember feeling like I had to look pretty, thin, and white. I remember thinking that being attractive (to boys) was the most important thing. I remember being in the closet about my bisexuality, being a Korean girl in a mostly white school, being fat, and being afraid to be myself. I remember feeling powerless to stand up to the things that made me feel small and all the things that seemed unfair about my world.

I also remember when I realized that I had a voice I could use to speak up for others and for myself. I remember when I came to understand that I could be beautiful without changing a thing about myself. I remember knowing in my gut when something was wrong and wanting to change it for the better. I remember turning my early passions for volunteering and helping people into a crusade for social justice. I am still that girl. I am that woman today.

There have been a lot of changes, but girls today are still up against a lot of biases and misperceptions. From a young age, girls are taught through popular media and toys that their worth is

ACTIVISM MEANS TAKING ACTION TO SUPPORT OR OPPOSE A CAUSE AND BRING ABOUT CHANGE.

linked to their appearance and what others think of them. By contrast, boys are taught that their worth is based on their accomplishments and abilities. Society makes girls feel like they have to change themselves to be accepted, that the surface is more important than the depth.

These messed-up notions are part of a chain reaction of inequity that results in girls and women being more likely to experience depression and loss of confidence. Girls and women also more likely to earn less money and live in poverty. We have fewer powerful female role models to look up to, less access to resources, and reduced rights under the law. That's just *wrong*.

When girls choose to speak out, we're demanding to be taken seriously. When girls care about issues, we show that we are vital members of society. When girls fight back against discrimination and harassment, we send the message that we'll stand up for ourselves no matter the consequences. When girls fight on behalf of others, we make it clear that we won't stand for injustice anywhere. The world needs girls' voices rising in protest. It needs girls organizing the girl resistance.

The world needs you!

Power Up

THE Girl

Resistance

From Joan of Arc (and probably way earlier) to Malala Yousafzai, girls and women have always led resistance movements. This is no coincidence: girls understand inequality because we experience it our whole lives. We get stuff done because we know no one else will do it for us. We speak out when we can no longer be silent. We support one another because we know important work can't get done alone. Girls resist because we care, because we're mad, because we're smart, and because we're powerful.

LET'S POWER UP! >

"I believe that words are easy. I believe the truth is told in the actions we take. And I believe that if enough ordinary people back up our desire for a better world with action, I believe we can, in fact, accomplish absolutely extraordinary things."

JODY WILLIAMS, American activist and Nobel Peace Prize winner

My mom used to say, "KaeLyn is always rooting for the underdog" because I've always been drawn to helping kids who are having a hard time. I spoke up to bullies. I didn't—and still don't—believe that anyone deserves to be treated unfairly. Maybe you believe that too.

As I grew up, life got more complicated. I felt pressure to fit in, to be the right kind of pretty, to be popular. But I always felt a little different—a Korean person in a mostly white town, an adoptee, a queer girl in the closet, a brainiac who always doubted her looks. So I naturally felt compassion for others, especially outsiders like me.

I was also a "joiner," and one of the school clubs I joined set up volunteer opportunities in our community—everything from picking up roadside trash to packing boxes at a food bank to tutoring young students. My friends and I started to help at a soup kitchen. During my first shift, when I was thirteen, a woman came in with two children, younger than I was. It shocked me. As the daughter of working middle-class parents, I had never been hungry, I had never been homeless. I went to school with kids who struggled with safe housing and access to basic needs, but I'd just never seen it firsthand. I had no words to describe what I was feeling, but I know now that I was confronting my **class privilege,** the set of advantages (a house, regular meals, clothes) that came with the income level of my family. For years I volunteered at that soup kitchen, and I got to know many of the people who came in for meals. I found my passion for volunteering, which set me up to stumble heart-first into feminist activism.

We live in scary times. Natural resources are being wasted, poisoned, or obliterated. World leaders are openly hateful toward women and girls, Black and brown people, immigrants, Muslims, and those who are transgender, gay, lesbian, or bisexual. Marginalized people fear violence at the hands of those who are supposed to protect them.

Lives are at stake.

If you have no idea how to understand or stand up against the social and political problems that keep heaping up, knowing where to start can be confusing, overwhelming, and exhausting. But you've already taken that important first step: *you're here.*

Maybe you opened this book because you're ready to become an activist. Maybe you're already an activist and want to grow and focus your skills. Maybe you've always known in your heart that there are other passionate, brave, smart girls out there and you want to tap into the power of girl resistance. Maybe you're just tired of being told your clothes are not appropriate at school, or being called mean names online, or being ignored when you speak up in class. No matter why you opened this book, I'm glad you're here.

In this chapter you will read about the ways that inequality manifests for girls and women today, what it means to be a grassroots organizer, and how to go out there and make change.

It's time to get stuff done!

Activism 101
Grassroots Power vs. Institutional Power

Activism means taking action to support or oppose a cause and bring about change. At its most abstract, activism is about creating shifts in power that benefit more people. To understand what activism means in practice, we need to understand and unpack the different kinds of power that exist.

Grassroots organizing is rooted—no pun intended—in the power of people, regular people, people like you. This type of activism is run by a group. It's social change at its most DIY. Grassroots movements use power in numbers to stand up to people or organizations that have **institutional power**, or power that comes through or with a job, position, money, identity, or status. What's that mean exactly? Here are some examples:

- The U.S. president has a lot of institutional power over every person living in the United States.

- Teachers have institutional power over students at school.

- The principal has power over the teachers and the students.

- A CEO has a power over a company's employees.

Why are these examples true? Most institutions (the school, the company, the United States) operate based on a hierarchical structure. In other words, in order to function in an orderly way, institutions need some people to be able to tell other people what to do.

In a school, a teacher needs to have power over students to make them do their homework, or else no one ever would (except maybe that one kid who's always like "you forgot to give us the assignment!"). The difference between the teacher's power and the students' power is called **structural inequity**, and that is what creates institutional power. It's easy to see how the structure works in a school: principal directs teachers; teachers make students take tests and do homework. But in society, the structures can be less visible or obvious. And something called **privilege** also influences which people in society have power.

Everyone has characteristics that make up who they are. Privilege is the power given to those who have the characteristics of the dominant group—not because they asked for that power, but because it's available to them. **Structural privilege** is about how much influence and power that society affords a person based on factors determined by social, political, and cultural values.

It can be difficult to change people's mindset when they've grown up having certain beliefs drilled into them. Understand their contexts, and think of what new approaches would create change.

SARNEET SARAN, teen mental-health activist

Who Has the Power?

Power can be based on race, ethnicity, gender, sexual orientation, religion, the amount of money someone has, their job or position, their education level, how they dress or act, and lots of other factors.

Look at the people on the opposite page. Who do you think has the most power? Did you focus first on the white man in the suit? If so, why do you think he has the most power? What makes you think he has structural privilege?

Who do you think has the least power? Did you choose the baby? What qualities make you think that?

Now look at the rest of the people and think about how they compare in terms of structural power and privilege. Some have power in certain ways but not in others. Who has more or less power than you, and in what ways?

This exercise shows that, maybe even without knowing, you already understand privilege and power dynamics. You didn't learn it by studying; you more likely learned it just by living in your daily life. Think about:

- Things you've seen or read or been exposed to that help you know what structural power looks like

- Your own life experiences that have shown you who has power and who doesn't

- Times when you've felt powerful

- Times when you've felt powerless

We learn about power, about who matters more or has more influence, and about what our cultures value most, in lots of little, subtle everyday ways. Every time we watch a movie where the main character is a girl who is saved by a boy, we get the message that boys are stronger than girls. Every time we read a book about a family with a mom and a dad, we get the message that families with single parents or gay or lesbian parents are less "normal." Every time we watch a TV show where all the main actors are white, we get the message that white people's stories are the most important.

THE POWER OF THE PEOPLE

Look at the picture of the baby again. What happens if she cries? A grown-up may have more power, but a crying baby will cry until a grown-up comes to pick her up. Even though she has less structural power than the grown-up, if the baby makes enough noise, the grown-up *has* to listen. That's how grassroots organizing works!

Grassroots organizing builds movements for change by bringing regular people together to raise their voices against groups with more structural power. For example, if all the students in your school banded together—to protest an unfair dress code, say—the united message will be hard for the principal to ignore. That's grassroots power. That's the *power of the people.*

It's not enough just to be one of many people who are upset about injustice. All the girls in your school might agree that the dress code is sexist, but that doesn't mean anything will happen to change it. Unless you *organize* to change it. By raising your voices collectively, it's more likely your voices will be heard, even when the people in power don't want to listen.

In this book, you'll learn about activist skills and strategies to organize for change, to wield *your* power as an activist in the girl resistance. But first, let's dive deeper into some girl-specific examples of how privilege and power work against us. (I promise it doesn't all suck.)

It's Not Easy Being a Girl

Now that we've covered the basics of activism, let's dig into the *why* behind it. The girl resistance is here because there's a lot of unfairness girls need to fight back against. It's important for girls to lead their own revolution because *it isn't easy being a girl*.

The system is stacked against us in a whole bunch of ways—which we'll get into soon—but all of them stem from the type of society that most of us live in. That society is known as a **patriarchy**.

Patriarchy is a system in which men have the most power in all areas of political, social, and cultural control. The United States of America and most of the world is led by patriarchal governments and societies. Patriarchy may not be an institution that has a literal, headquarters, but it holds the kind of institutional power that keeps people in a hierarchy—with women much lower than men.

Obviously, we've come a long way since the days when women couldn't vote, work outside the home, or choose whom to marry. But just because we've won some victories doesn't mean there aren't battles left to fight. Patriarchy still exists, but it's not as in-your-face as not allowing women to show their bare ankles or preventing women from owning property (both of which used to be a thing). But it's definitely there.

Let's walk through the life of a girl and see all the ways sexist inequality chips away at our personhood, and how we can take action and fight back.

GENDER NORMS

From infancy, girls are treated differently from boys because of **gender,** that is, whether a person is male or female. It starts in the way that adults talk to and treat us. Little girls are more likely to be complimented for being pretty and sweet, while little boys are more likely to be praised for being tough and strong. Girls are taught to be polite, quiet, and caring, while boys are encouraged to be assertive, tough, and physically active. Toys made for girls tend to focus on cleaning and cooking, taking care of baby dolls, clothing and fashion; they promote nurturing qualities. Toys made for boys are things like cars and trucks and science sets and model kits, promoting problem-solving and building skills. A little girl can imagine herself doing almost anything . . . as long as it takes place inside her home—having babies and cleaning and putting on makeup. A boy is encouraged to imagine being an astronaut or athlete or firefighter.

These differences are based on **gender norms,** the stereotypes about what is supposed to be natural and appropriate based on a person's gender. Even if your parents didn't impose these stereotypes on you, gender norms are everywhere. Think about the magazines sold to girls, most of which are full of fashion, diets, and gossip, versus those for boys, all about power, cars, and sex. Gender norms even come through in something as small as a man holding a door open for a woman—it's just expected that women need help.

These ideas and assumptions can be hard to notice because gender norms are just that—normal. We're accustomed to them. If you love stereotypically "girly" stuff, that's totally fine! I love makeup and dresses, too. There's nothing wrong with liking things that align with gender norms, if that's truly how you feel. In fact, it can be really powerful to reclaim those things for yourself. Only when gender norms become mandatory, when we feel like we have to follow these rules, do they become unfairly restrictive.

Gender norms also enforce the idea of the **gender binary**, meaning the idea that there are only two possible genders—boy and girl, man and woman, male and female. However, there are many other gender identities out there. Definitely more than two. More like two dozen (and probably even more than that)! Some people identify as **gender fluid**: on any given day they may feel more like a girl, or more like a boy, or somewhere in between. Others are **gender expansive** or **gender nonbinary**; their gender doesn't fit rigidly into any one box.

Kids and adults experience gender identity and expression in lots of different ways, but gender norms keep everyone in one small, narrowly defined box. The female gender norm box tells us we have to be quiet, focus on looking attractive, and always be less smart and less powerful than boys. That box can suffocate us if those traits aren't our own—which is the case for most girls. But we can push our way out and demand to be taken seriously and treated fairly.

FIGHT BACK!

Cross Out Gender Norms: Get friends or a group together and have a T-shirt-making party. Using fabric markers, write "I am" followed by a stereotypical "girl" trait. For example: "I am polite" or "I am gentle" or "I am pretty." Then cross out the trait and write below it something more personal and positive, like "smart" or "strong" or "fierce" or "powerful" or "confident" or "unique." Wear your shirts on the same day and post pics on social media to further your reach!

Confront the Dress Code: Does your school enforce a sexist dress code that restricts clothes that girls can wear (for example, unreasonable rules banning spaghetti straps or skirts that go above the knee because they would be "distracting" to boys)? Are the rules different for girls and boys? Are trans or gender-nonconforming students able to wear the clothes that are right for them? Use petition, protest, and/or media exposure to raise awareness of why these sexist rules are offensive and demand that your school change its dress code.

Break the Binary: In how you speak, that is. Train yourself to use language that is inclusive of gender-nonbinary people. Practice it. Memorize it. Teach it to others. Here are some examples:

INSTEAD OF SAYING:	SAY:
"men and women"	"everyone"
"ladies and gentlemen"	"distinguished guests"
"his or hers"	"theirs"
"that girl/guy with the black hair"	"that person with the black hair"
"Ma'am" or "Sir"	"Pardon me, please"

I know what it is to live in a deep loneliness and fear. I know what it is to be ritualistically misunderstood, ignored, and targeted. Girls like me across the world know this reality all too well. The mistreatment and harming of trans and nonbinary people of color has been legislated. It's enculturated. It's directed. It's even too often required. That is why I fight.

SAGE GRACE DOLAN-SANDRINO, teen Afro-Latina transgender actress, writer, journalist, and activist

THE CONFIDENCE GAP

Think about all the men you've learned about in school. Authors, world leaders, scientists, poets, and more. Now think of all the women. How many can you even name? In our society, boys can easily imagine a future where they can be anything because they've learned about men who've done everything. Girls have to imagine their future without many role models and without the structural power that comes from being male. We end up comparing ourselves to men, and since the only successful people we learn about are men, many of us subconsciously believe that we aren't as capable of success.

> **GIRLHOOD IS SISTERHOOD AND SISTERHOOD IS TREATING ONE ANOTHER LIKE FAMILY, PULLING OTHERS UP, STANDING TOGETHER.**

All these small feelings of self-doubt add up to feeling super inadequate—and it starts early. According to a 2017 study published by the American Association for the Advancement of Science, five-year-old girls are just as likely to think of girls and boys as "brilliant." But by age six, when shown pictures of men and women, girls are less likely to choose women as brilliant. Boys chose their gender as "really, really smart" 65 percent of the time. Girls chose their gender only 48 percent of the time!

This confidence gap continues into adulthood. A 2015 study of adult men and women in 48 countries found that, regardless of continent or culture, women ranked their self-esteem lower than men did. This is a huge problem, and not just because having low self-esteem feels crummy. The less confident you feel, the less likely you are to seek jobs or positions that may seem daunting. The fewer women in influential, decision-making positions, the less women's interests and well-being are taken into consideration by people in power.

The confidence gap won't be fixed just by encouraging girls to be smart and strong and active and all that other inspirational meme stuff, though that's one place to start. It won't be fixed until there is a level playing field between men and women, until women have as much structural power as men. We have to encourage each other not to be afraid to step into leadership roles, to be powerful and out in the world fiercely creating our futures. Girls must refuse to compete with each other, as we're often encouraged to do.

Girlhood is sisterhood and sisterhood is treating one another like family, pulling others up, standing together, and resisting every day.

FIGHT BACK!

Create Feminist Social Groups: A powerful way to beat back negative self-talk is to surround yourself with smart, caring girls. You'll feel stronger together and have someone safe to talk to when you feel insecure or upset. Make friends on social media or by getting involved with a feminist or activist leadership program.

Form Intergenerational Connections: Work with a local women's business association, women's leadership organization, or feminist group that pairs teen girls with older women for mentoring, career advice, job shadowing, or just having a cup of coffee. Or host an intergenerational panel of girls and women speaking about their experiences with sexism and self-confidence.

Invest in Yourself: Activism isn't always outward-facing—sometimes it's working on ourselves so we can be better people. Have body image issues? Follow body-positive women on social media; say something nice about yourself every time you look in the mirror. Figure out what you feel most insecure about and then confront it head-on!

IMPLICIT BIAS

Humans are just that—human. Even with good intentions, we make subtle judgments based on stereotypes that limit possibilities for others or for ourselves. Anyone of any gender can do any job—obviously—but it's harder in a patriarchy when old-fashioned (and, obviously, totally wrong) ideas about what jobs women and men are good at are widespread. When a woman applies for a STEAM job, like an engineer position, she's less likely to get it than a man with similar qualifications. Why? Because gender stereotypes assume that she is less skilled no matter how awesome her résumé is. She's at a disadvantage because of the preconceived notion that women are better suited to domestic or caregiving work. Does this mean the hiring manager is a bad, sexist person? Not necessarily—they may just have a gut feeling that a male candidate would be better, and they may act on it without realizing or understanding it.

This kind of unconscious discrimination is called **implicit bias**. Implicit bias can be based on any facet of identity, such as race, gender, sexuality, religion, or ability. Some studies show that toddlers absorb implicit bias about racial prejudice as early as three years old!

Implicit bias about gender stereotypes has real, measurable effects on the lives of girls, even as early as elementary school. A teacher doesn't have to literally say "girls can't do math"; they don't even have to know that they hold that belief for it to be damaging. Teachers who do not consciously address their implicit bias about girls' ability in math are much more likely to treat girls as less competent—and research has shown that such negative stereotypes can result in lower test scores. But when girls and boys are told that they're equally capable (which, of course, they actually are), the difference in test scores disappears.

Implicit bias affects people of many (if not most) marginalized identities. The prejudice that, in intelligence, white kids are the norm and Asian kids are super smart and hardworking, results in Black, Latinx, and other kids of color getting less feedback and attention at school. The assumption that a woman wearing hijab is oppressed causes people to regard her with suspicion when she's shopping at a store or walking down the street.

Combatting implicit bias means pushing back on all the preconceived gender norms we talked about earlier, but it also means just being aware that implicit bias exists. We can't send out effective countermessaging until we dig up what the damaging messages are. Most of all, we need to mean it when we say that girls can do anything, no matter what it is.

FIGHT BACK!

Test Yourself: Learning about your own biases can help you be a better activist because you can take steps to actively *unlearn* those biases. But how do you unlearn something that's unconscious? Try taking the implicit bias tests at Project Implicit (implicit.harvard .edu), available in many languages and covering topics from sexual orientation to disability to various racial and ethnic groups. You may be surprised what associations your brain makes unconsciously!

Girls' Science Fair: Plan one in your school or neighborhood. Or volunteer to do an easy science project with younger girls, like making glow-in-the-dark or glitter slime! You can find tons of recipes online.

I Am Not a Stereotype Project: Call out stereotypes through a social media campaign. Encourage people to take selfies and post how they break stereotypes with the hashtag #iamnotastereotype. Or create posters depicting people who break biases and stereotypes and hang them around your school (with permission) to start the conversation.

THE GENDER WAGE GAP

Guess what? This stuff doesn't get better when you grow up! Back in the day, women weren't even allowed to do certain jobs—newspaper ads used to be separated into a women's section and a men's section. Needless to say, with no way to get a foot in the door, women had a super hard time excelling in those fields (though some radical, hard-fighting women did, and they were totally awesome).

Thankfully (and thanks to some of those trailblazing ladies), women and men in many parts of the world now have access to the same jobs, and in the United States discrimination on the basis of sex is illegal. Somehow, though, in practically every field, women earn less than men. For the exact same work. *Still.* In 2015, women earned 20 percent less than men. So for every $1 a man makes, a woman is paid 80 cents. The breakdown is worse for people of color:

- Black women are paid 63 cents for every $1 a white man makes.

- Hispanic women and Latinas earn only 54 cents for every $1 a white man makes.

- Across races and ethnicities, women of color earn less than men of color (who, in turn, make less than white men).

Other factors that can affect women's pay include if they have a disability, their sexual orientation, gender identity, and age. In 2015, people with disabilities made 68 percent of what people without disabilities made. And women with disabilities made 69 percent of what men with disabilities made. Trans women earn less than their male colleagues and actually see a decrease in pay after they come out. Lesbian and bisexual women make less than their male colleagues, including gay and bisexual men. (And in many places in the United States, employers can openly discriminate against transgender people and others based on sexual orientation.)

Why does this matter so much? Because we live in a capitalist society, where money = power. Because women don't make as much money, they are more likely than men to experience poverty at every age. We will continue to bring in less money in retirement because social assistance and safety-net money for retired and elderly folks are based on what you earned while working.

PAY INEQUITY ISN'T JUST ABOUT HAVING LESS CASH TO BUY STUFF: IT'S ANOTHER FORM OF STRUCTURAL INEQUALITY THAT AFFECTS OUR WHOLE LIVES.

Plus, there's the issue of unpaid work: in a study of heterosexual couples, women spent twice as much time on chores as their male partners—often on top of work outside the home—and they're not paid for it. In a capitalist society, we equate the "value" of an action with "literal money received for doing it," so basically society is saying that all that housekeeping, cooking, cleaning, and childcare that women perform—which is *definitely* work—is worth nothing. Considering everything women do inside *and* outside the home, it's outrageous that we're still paid less than men.

FiGHT BACK!

Gender-Bender Bake Sale: Raise awareness of the gender wage gap with a gender-bender bake sale! It's like a regular bake sale, except that men pay different prices than women: for example, a man pays $1 for a cupcake, but woman will pay 75 cents for that same cupcake (rounded down from 80 cents because who wants to deal with making change?). Unfair? Sure—that's the point. Use the sale as an opportunity to tell folks that the difference is even greater for Black women and Latinas.

Girls' Career Day: Plan one at your school. Invite professional women to talk about their jobs and the ways that gender inequity has impacted their careers, as well as to give advice to girls who want to enter their field one day. Invite women from all professions, especially traditionally male-dominated jobs like doctors, engineers, scientists, lawyers, and CEOs.

Promote Equal Pay Day: This is the day that women's wages finally catch up with men's from the previous year. So, for example, if this year's Equal Pay Day is in April, that means that women had to work until April to make as much as men made by the previous December. Equal Pay Day is celebrated around the world. The date changes based on the country's previous year's stats. Google "Equal Pay Day" to find the date. Organize a protest or set up a table with literature. Do anything to raise awareness of the pay gap.

Black women are the cornerstone of our communities, we are phenomenal, and we deserve equal pay.

LAVERNE COX, Emmy-nominated actress and transgender trailblazer on Black Women's Equal Pay Day (July 31, 2017)

LACK OF WOMEN IN GOVERNMENT

We're all well aware that the United States has never had a female president. But women have been successful leaders since the beginning of recorded human history, from Cleopatra to Elizabeth II. As of this book's publication, 15 women are currently national leaders and 59 countries have had a woman leader in the past half decade, according to the World Economic Forum.

Still, women make up a small percentage of political leaders and of elected officials at all levels of government around the world. In the U.S., women make up slightly more than 50 percent of the population, but hold

- less than 20 percent of seats in Congress
- less than 25 percent of seats in state legislatures
- less than 20 percent of mayoral seats

As of 2017, 38 women of color (18 Black, 10 Latina, 9 Asian or Pacific Islander, 1 multiracial) serve in Congress, and 61 women of color have ever served in U.S. history. One openly lesbian woman, Tammy Baldwin, serves in the Senate. One openly bisexual woman, and the first bisexual woman to win, Kyrsten Sinema, serves in the House of Representatives.

Sure, we've come a long way—in 1971, only 3 percent of U.S. Congressional seats were held by women. (I know, that's really bad!) But we still have a long way to go. The U.S. currently ranks 101st for gender parity in parliament (or Congress, as we call it here), meaning we have a smaller percentage of women in our legislative elective body than 100 other countries. Rwanda has the highest percentage of women in parliament. Cuba, Iceland, and Nicaragua have almost reached gender parity (an equal number of women and men in office). In other words, women in U.S. government are way behind most of the world.

Remember when we defined patriarchy on page 21? This is what it looks like in practice: men literally having more power over the entire country, the system of government, the laws and policies—and, thus, over women's and girls' lives.

The good news is, today women are running for office in record numbers. In the days after the 2016 U.S. presidential election, organizations that train women to run for office were flooded with interest. New mentorship programs have popped up. Recent election cycles have proved that women are the future mayors, governors, senators, and, yes, presidents that will lead American forward.

WE HAVE TO FIND OUR OWN ROLE MODELS, SUPPORT EACH OTHER IN LEADERSHIP POSITIONS, AND MAKE THE ISSUES AND VOICES OF GIRLS HEARD IN ELECTIONS.

In fact, in the 2017 elections, women positively rocked the vote, winning in record numbers *everywhere*. In Virginia alone, the first Asian woman, first two Latina women, first openly lesbian woman, and first openly trans woman joined the state's House of Delegates. Andrea Jenkins became the first openly transgender person of color to win public office when she picked up a seat on the Minneapolis city council. A twentysomething female college grad picked up a city council seat in Aurora, Colorado, taking down the 79-year-old male incumbent. Seattle elected its first openly lesbian mayor. Charlotte, North Carolina, elected its first Black woman mayor. And New Jersey got its first Black lieutenant governor. That's, like, unprecedentedly awesome stuff!

But there are still lots of challenges for us. We have to find our own role models, support each other in leadership positions, and make the issues and voices of girls important in elections.

FIGHT BACK!

Call or Walk for a Woman Candidate: Even if you're not old enough to vote, you're old enough to volunteer for a campaign—in fact, short of voting, personal outreach is one of the most effective ways you can help elect a candidate. Get in touch with the campaign manager, and they'll have you volunteering in no time! Bring friends to make it extra fun. Keep those skills in mind when you run for office in a few years (wink, wink).

Throw a House Party: Passionate about a female candidate? Throw a fundraiser and awareness raiser. Invite your friends, family, everyone you can think of. Keep it affordable so young people can attend, serve snacks and drinks, and contact the candidate's campaign team for materials to hang or distribute. And be sure to let your candidate know about the party—she may want to stop by!

Get Out the Vote: Whether or not you're old enough to vote, you can help make sure other people do their civic duty! Share voting-rights info on social media. Volunteer for a campaign to make phone calls reminding people to vote. If you have a car and a driver's license, volunteer to give rides to the polls on election day. (Just bring a trusted adult along for safety.)

We're half the people—we should be half the Congress.

JEANETTE RANKIN, first female member of the U.S. Congress

GIRLS' SEXUALITY AND RAPE CULTURE

Barbie dolls. Bratz dolls. Monster High dolls. Some of our earliest lessons about how girls are supposed to behave and what we're supposed to look like take place via the toys and consumer goods marketed to young girls. More often than not, these products are **hypersexualized**. Hypersexualization doesn't mean that girls are being forced to have sex or to be sexual. Sexualization is a cultural idea that girls' attractiveness is based on our ability to be sexy, and that, in turn, our worth is based on how attractive we are. Hypersexualization is this idea taken to an extreme.

Hypersexualization can also lead girls to self-sexualize: to believe that our worth is based on our attractiveness as defined by what other people think is sexy. This leads to anxiety about appearance, which can result in depression, low self-esteem, and low self-worth.

Hypersexualization affects Black girls in particular. A recent study found that Black girls are viewed as being more "grown up" and "less innocent" than white girls. This stereotype can lead to the perception that Black girls know more about sex and adult topics, need less support and nurturing, and are more independent. And all *that* can lead to Black girls enduring harsher penalities at school while having lower self-esteem, on average.

For all girls, the sexualizing of girlhood comes down to a very complicated and disgusting aspect of patriarchal society known as **rape culture**. Rape culture is a set of social and cultural ideas, images, practices, and institutions that promote the normalizing of sexual violence against women.

While young girls learn that their sexuality is the most valuable thing about them, boys learn that girls are sexual objects for *their* pleasure, that girls' bodies are to be stared at, talked about, rated, and touched—with no regard for the girls' feelings or experiences.

Even well-meaning statements as innocent as "He's just mean to you because he likes you" can instill the idea that male aggression against women is acceptable (or even cute—ugh).

Even though it can start with playground antics and rude comments, the consequences of rape culture are extremely serious. According to the Rape, Abuse, and Incest National Network (RAINN), 1 in 9 children under the age of 18 experiences sexual assault by an adult, and 82 percent of sexual assault survivors under age 18 are girls.

Another part of rape culture is the belief that girls are responsible for sexual harassment, abuse, and assault. If a girl is "good," she won't have sex. So if a girl is raped, it's because she isn't a "good girl." She didn't protect herself or communicate what she wanted or wear the right clothes (never mind the fact that women have been assaulted while wearing everything from overalls to turtlenecks). The pressure is always on girls not to get raped, not on rapists *not to rape*—which is absolutely ridiculous. ("He should have known that owning a Playstation was just asking for someone to steal it!" Like, come on.) Girls are told to be virginal and chaste while simultaneously being exposed over and over to hypersexual culture. These mixed messages are enough to make your eyes cross—or seriously piss you off (both acceptable reactions).

Be assertive and speak your mind! Don't constrain yourself by being what society deems a "nice girl."

ANNA GARRISON-BEDELL, teen intersectional feminist
who fights racism, sexism, income inequality, and homophobia

Reach Out for Help

If you were abused or assaulted, you are not alone. I was sexually assaulted when I was 18 and in college. It happens to too many girls and women. If you want to talk to someone confidentially or find resources in your area, call or chat online with someone at RAINN right now (rainn.org). The most cruel and devastating impact of rape culture is that it promotes and sustains a society in which girls are disproportionately affected by sexual violence every single day. Seek the help you need to deal with it.

We fight rape culture and hypersexualization by taking back control of our bodies and sexual selves. Once we recognize what's happening around us, we can decide for ourselves how to dress, whom to date and have sexual relationships with, and what feels right for our own bodies. Whether you choose to wear baggy jeans or miniskirts, long hair or a buzz cut, no makeup or bright-red lipstick, to have sex or not, how you express your sexuality belongs to you. You're nobody's sex object.

FIGHT BACK!

Yes Means Yes: Our culture spends so much time telling teens not to have sex. But people rarely talk about how to say "Yes!" to the sex we want or how to get consent from a partner in a sexual situation. Invite a sex educator to your school or youth group to give a talk on consent. Or before your next prom or homecoming dance, organize an "I respect consent" pledge and ask students to sign it.

Get Good Sex Ed: Does your school offer comprehensive sex education? Comprehensive sex ed includes teaching elementary children about bodily autonomy and the right not to be touched by adults; teaches teens how to prevent pregnancy and sexually transmitted infections; provides information for queer and trans teens; educates students about consent and sexual communication; and offers bystander intervention skills to help people take action when they see someone in danger. If not, ask for it. Use resources like Scarleteen (scarleteen.com) to guide curriculum design. Or, if you can't get it through official channels, start a peer sex-ed group (which can be as casual as just chatting with your friends).

Create Care Kits for Survivors of Rape: Find a rape crisis provider in your area and see if they accept donated "care kits" of toiletries, makeup, and clothing for sexual assault survivors. Often, if the person goes to the emergency room for a sexual assault forensic exam ("rape kit"), they need a comfortable change of clothes and some basic products to help them feel human again. Collect items at your school, church, or community center.

Stand Up! Rise Up! Fight Back!

So what can *you* do when your rights are under attack? Stand up! Rise up! Fight back! RESIST.

Where to begin? It probably makes your brain explode just thinking about everything that's messed up. The good news is we're smart, strong, and resilient. We have to be.

We're also optimistic. We believe it will get better. In our lifetimes! How do things get better? We make them better.

We stand up for our own rights and the rights of other people. We don't back down in the face of those in power who want to pass laws and rules that hurt us. We demand to be listened to and refuse to be silenced. We are half the world's population and we deserve to be treated equally. That's it. Full stop.

We won't change it all overnight. We can't individually end all unfairness in the world. We start by doing something to fight back, putting good back into the world, individually committing to working for a better future. We start by building power, by building the girl resistance within our communities. As more and more girls take control of their futures and work to better the world around us, we'll win together.

That is what the girl resistance looks like: a generation of girls speaking up, standing for what's right, shouting out, demanding justice for all, supporting each other, leading the way, and not letting the system shut us down.

Are you ready to resist?

☆ ☆ ☆ ☆ # Takeaways ☆ ☆ ☆ ☆ ☆

1 Activism is about taking action to create shifts in power that benefit more people.

What ways have you experienced the collective "power of the people," or grassroots organizing? How can you use your voice, combined with the voices of others, to push back against hierarchies, unfair laws, and other forms of institutional oppression in your school or community? Try to put some of those ideas into action to bring about positive change.

2 Girls and women experience a lot of oppression, simply because of their gender.

What adult women do you know who have experienced unequal pay or inequity in the workplace? What did they do about it? Do you ever find yourself thinking along gender-binary lines? How can you open yourself up to seeing beyond gender stereotypes and the implicit biases they create?

3 You don't have to be powerful to join the girls resist movement.

Grassroots organizing and activism are all about ordinary people rising up together to create power and use that power to effect change. Work on crafting your vision for a better world and get started!

Creating

(AND CRUSHING)

Your First

Campaign Plan

Maybe you feel overwhelmed by all the problems and conditions in your hometown, region, country, or the world that are unfair and horrible and ought to be changed. With so many competing injustices deserving of support, you might be wondering where to start. In this chapter, you'll learn how to pick a cause, set goals, and identify people who can help. Are you ready?

LET'S DO THIS THING! ❯

"All of us [are] driven by a simple belief that the world as it is simply won't do—that we have an obligation to fight for the world as it should be."

MICHELLE OBAMA, African American First Lady of the United States

The best way to kick-start your activist career is by focusing on one or two areas that you can fully commit your energy to. That's not to say you shouldn't care about all the problems out there. You should totally care! Caring about fairness and equity is what makes you a good person and a good activist.

But let's explore how to build a campaign around the *one* cause you are able to tackle *right now*. Why? Because it's impossible to work on all the issues at once. If you do, you may end up feeling totally overwhelmed and could eventually suffer from "activist burnout"—the physical and emotional exhaustion that comes from overworking yourself. (Read more about battling this type of fatigue in Chapter 8.)

You will have the most impact and the most energy to make lasting change if you choose one place to start your activism. Then, when you want to start another project or campaign, you'll be ready to tackle it head-on.

Picking Your Activist Issue:
The Mind Map

The hardest part about planning a campaign is knowing where to start, because the flip side of "you can do anything!" is that you can also do *everything*, which would be exhausting and impossible. You've gotta narrow it down!

Enter the **mind map**. This cool visual tool can help you get all those jumbly thoughts out of your brain and start to make sense of them. Mind maps are nonlinear, which means they don't follow a rigid structure like a chart or graph, and you can use them for all sorts of tasks, from decision making and project planning to taking notes for a class. In this case, we're going to create one to help you select an activist issue. You can use the blank mind map on the opposite page or draw your own.

In the center bubble of the mind map, draw an image that represents activism to you, such as a megaphone or a paintbrush or a rally sign or a stick-figure drawing of yourself in an extremely fierce outfit. Drawing pictures might feel silly, but it helps unlock the creative side of your brain and encourages the free flow of ideas.

Next, in the smaller bubbles, write or draw the causes or issues you care about. Add more bubbles if you need to. Don't overthink it, just write whatever pops into your head. Use colorful markers or pens or scribble in black ink—whatever you want.

Now, around each bubble, write why you care about that issue and how you would change it if you had unlimited resources. Write everything that comes to mind. Sketch a line from each reason and idea back to the issue in the smaller bubble. Do this for each one.

THE MIND MAP

Use this template or make your own to create your personalized activism mind map

1. START WITH AN IMAGE THAT REPRESENTS ACTIVISM TO YOU
2. ADD ISSUES YOU CARE ABOUT
3. FILL LINES WITH WHY YOU CARE

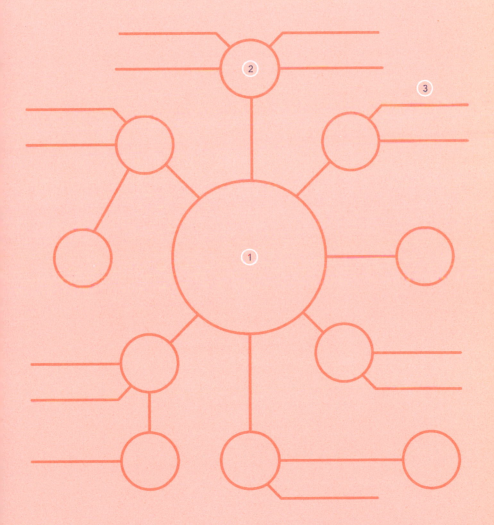

Look at your map. Which one or two bubbles have the most lines around them? Which do you feel most passionate about? Pick that as the issue at the heart of your campaign, the one you will think about a lot, and the one for which you're going to work hard to affect change. Do something visual to make clear that this is your #1 issue: Draw lots of stars or hearts around it. Circle it in highlighter or thick black marker. Make a little collage. You're going to go hard on this sucker.

For the other issues in your map—the ones you're not going to tackle in your campaign—think about one small, concrete way you can support each one, so that you don't feel like you're abandoning them when you turn your focus to your main issue. Make one more line off each nonpriority issue and write one simple action, like "donate money" or "sign a petition" or "share online." Draw a star or smiley face or whatever symbolizes "Yes. Cool. I can do this" to you. Remember: when it comes to activism, following is just as important as leading.

That's it! The mind map is complete. Nice work. Display or keep your mind map somewhere you'll see it every day and let it inspire you to make change.

Do I *have* to make a mind map?

Totally not. If you already know what you want to tackle—or if you see a news story, tweet, or post that super-pisses you off—run with it. Especially if it's recent and time-sensitive (like a bill in your state that discriminates against trans people, for example). Get right to the campaign plan, girl!

Making a Campaign Plan

Now that you've chosen your issue, you need to plan how you're going to make change. A common next step is coming up with a short-term idea to "do something" without any big-picture planning—identifying the *what* before defining the *why*. Many spontaneous activist moments led to incredible movement-building and change-making: the Stonewall Riots, Black Lives Matter, Occupy Wall Street, the Women's March on Washington.

If you want to sustain your efforts—and you will have to, because this stuff does not change overnight—you need a strategy. Start with, "I'm *super mad* about this and here is what needs to change."

Then define what that change, winning, or making progress looks like. This type of thinking, considering the long-term, big-picture process and all the nitty-gritty details, can be difficult for any activist. Introducing (dun-dun-dun!): the **campaign plan**.

A campaign plan is exactly what it sounds like. (And, admittedly, it doesn't sound super fun. Feel free to come up with a cooler name.) It's both your map and your compass—it'll help you envision success and plot a path to get there. By seeing the big picture as well as helping you make decisions or change direction during your campaign, it keeps you focused and pushes you to move beyond losses to the next phase. Consider your campaign plan a working document, meaning that you can change or update it at any time (say, when an election didn't go the way you hoped it would).

TL;DR: DON'T START WITH A PROTEST. START WITH A PLAN.

Defining Your Vision and Goals

A campaign plan starts with your **vision**. To determine what your vision is, ask yourself these two important questions:

Why do you want to tackle this issue?

What are you fighting for?

In other words, after you've achieved everything you're fighting for, what will the world ideally be like? In many cases, the vision is that your work or activism will no longer be needed—your world will be that much better. For example, if your cause is LGBTQ+ youth homelessness, a vision would be that every child has a safe and secure place to live, no matter their identity. That's a very clear and inspiring vision. But it's not a goal.

Many activists confuse vision with a goal. A vision is super-duper big—it's the *reason* you are doing this work. It reminds you what you're fighting for. It's the positive outcome if you win absolutely everything you want. A **goal** is *measurable* and *specific.* Goals need to be broken down into steps or phases to be achievable, so let's see how to do that.

The Main Goal

First, write down the one big thing you hope to accomplish—the measurable, attainable, concrete action you want to see happen.

For example, maybe you want to get a nondiscrimination bill passed, raise money for an after-school program, or change your school's mascot to your Siamese cat. Whatever! This is the *purpose* of your campaign. If you're 100 percent successful, this outcome is the goal you will achieve.

SHORT-TERM AND MEDIUM-TERM GOALS

These are the smaller objectives you need to complete along the way to your main goal. Let's say you're trying to get your school's sexist dress code changed. Here's how your smaller goals might build up:

- Educate others at school about your issue

- Get media (or social media) attention about your issue

- Get support from school board members or administrators

Notice that we're not listing *how* you'll do these things. Goals are all about the *what*, and having these smaller milestones figured out will help you determine the best, most efficient strategies and tactics—stuff like protests and petitions and fundraisers (all covered in the next chapter). But first, we need to figure out just *who* are the people you need to get on board to make change.

# Targets

Now that you know *what* you want to achieve—your goals—you have to figure out *who* can make it happen. You need to know who is standing in your way, who has the power to help you, or both. That's your **target,** and every campaign plan needs at least one.

Targets are *people* who have institutional power. That means, for example, your target can't be "the school," which is just a stack of bricks or pile of stones; but it can be a school board or principal or superintendent. Without a target, your activism doesn't truly have an aim. You'll just find yourself shouting into the void but, like, without anyone listening. So spare yourself the sore throat and make a list of targets.

You're probably thinking, *Okay, KaeLyn, easier said than done because how am I supposed to know who is in charge of . . . everything?*

Short answer: it'll all be based on your goals. The example of the sexist dress code is easy—with a little googling (or a peek in the school handbook), you can figure out who makes the decisions at your school. But if your goal is something bigger—like the so-called Bathroom Bill in North Carolina that discriminates against trans people—you'll suddenly have to remember everything you learned in middle-school gov class. Or maybe your target is another kind of powerful individual, like a CEO of a corporation or the owner of a small business. Or maybe you have no idea who is responsible for the crappy thing you want to change. UGH.

Don't sweat it. Here's a quick primer to help you identify some common targets who hold institutional power and therefore may be your ticket to success.

GOVERNMENT BIG WIGS

Have you ever wondered who makes the decisions that affect your town or city? Who decides what the speed limits are and how much money your parents pay in taxes? Who sets the rules that protect consumers from fraud or safeguard animals from abuse?

Lots of people do the work of legislating—making laws—at different levels of government. The elected officials that make up these legislatures ensure that the views and wishes of as many people as possible are represented and considered when drafting new laws or changing old ones.

Local: It is usually local elected officials who have the biggest impact on your community's daily life. That's because they're closest to their constituents, the people who elect them based on what they stand for, likely their neighbors or store owners or pastors or children's teachers.

There are several types of local legislatures, such as a city council or town/county board or village trustees. There's also a leader of your city, town, and/or county—a mayor or supervisor or person in charge. To learn what type of government your area has, google the name of your hometown and look for its official homepage. (Warning: expect some super-tacky web designs.)

State: Your state's legislature is made up of representatives and senators from—you guessed it—the state you live in. They pass laws that affect people and institutions in *only* your state. These law-making bodies draft and vote on bills they want to be made into laws. If the majority votes favorably on the bill, it proceeds to the state's executive branch—your governor. The governor can either sign the law into effect or veto it. The discriminatory Bathroom Bill mentioned earlier (officially known as House Bill 2) is a statewide law that affects only the residents of North Carolina.

Federal: The U.S. government is designed as a checks-and-balance system made up of three branches: the legislative branch (Congress), the executive branch (the president), and the judicial branch (the Supreme Court). It's pretty hard to get the president of the United States or the Supreme Court to listen to your case, but members of Congress are elected officials, just like the people who serve in your local legislatures. They work for *voters*—your family, teachers, neighbors, and everyone else you know and whose views you can influence. As in state government, laws typically start as bills, which are voted on by the House of Representatives and Senate before they land on the president's desk. U.S. representatives are elected based on population (so more populous states have more reps), whereas senators come in pairs (two per state, for every state).

International: Countries and communities all over the world have different systems of government, but most have some sort of a leader—a president or queen or emir or sovereign or some other fancy title—who may or may not be elected by the people. For obvious reasons, these folks are a little out of reach (but feel free to write Queen Elizabeth or Chancellor Angela Merkel a fan letter anyway).

PRIVATE POWERFUL PEOPLE

Nonprofits: These are just what they sound like: organizations that do not seek to earn profits. Nonprofits exist for the common good (or what they believe is the common good—you won't agree with every nonprofit's mission). They are run by a board of directors and led by an executive director, and they often have to make all their financial records (including how much money the director is paid) available to the public.

Corporations: These organizations are out to make money. Most stores, businesses, and media companies are corporations (though some are not; those have a slightly different legal designation, like an LLC). Corporations are owned by people, either an individual or a group, like a board of directors or shareholders or both. Corporations are typically led by a president or director. Their earnings and compensation do not have to be made public.

Local Businesses: These are a type of corporation, but if they're small and local, they're likely run by a few people or one person who is the owner and founder. They may have investors but typically don't have stockholders.

Media Companies: Media companies, like most magazines, blogs, newspapers, and radio/TV stations, are corporations that are typically run by a publisher or editor in chief and advised by a group of people called the editorial board.

How do they help you reach your targets?

Some of these target types might not have direct decision-making power over your issue but could still influence the people who do. Those are your *secondary* targets. For example, if your **primary target** is the mayor, **secondary targets** might be the city council that debates issues of local politics; local journalists who cover news in your area; or even a critical mass of constituents (remember, all politicians need votes to stay in office). If you get their support, they might help you convince the person in power to hear you out.

BIG-PICTURE TARGETS

But what if your whole campaign is about something really freaking big, like ending rape culture? Who has the power to end rape culture? Um, *everyone on earth pretty much*, amirite? For obvious reasons, that target is not clear (or manageable) enough. So dig deeper: Who *specifically* has the most power to end it? In this case, cisgender men and boys are the most complicit in perpetuating rape culture—so they also have the power to stop it.

But you may have to narrow it down even more: How about the boys in your school, the men in your family, or even a handful of male friends? You don't have to be personal—just do a little research. For example, if you read about women at a local company protesting the crappy sexual harassment policies they endure, the person with power is probably the CEO of that company. Voilà! A target appears!

> **SOMETIMES YOU NEED TO PICK A TARGET THAT IS SYMBOLIC OF A BIGGER GROUP BECAUSE IT WILL GIVE YOU SOMEWHERE TO AIM YOUR EFFORTS.**

To get back to the case study of a campaign in favor of changing your school's unfair dress code, the decision-making authority is probably the school board and student government. So your targets would be school board members and student government representatives. Boom. Done.

Rallying the Troops

You can't fight your battle alone! Well, you can . . . but it'll be a lot harder and kinda lonely. Also, some people are actively fighting against you, and there's power in numbers, so get as many numbers (aka people) on your side as possible. Once you have a vision, concrete goals, and specific targets—but *before* you charge onto the battlefield—it's a good idea to get the lay of the land.

FINDING ALLIES

Sometimes it's comforting and necessary to be surrounded by like-minded people—they will have your back, check your logic, provide support, and prompt you to think more critically. And when you're fighting for a cause, many of these people or groups will become your **allies**, partners in your cause. To determine who might make up this vital group, consider these simple questions:

Who already agrees with you?

Who is already doing similar work?

What supportive people and organizations might be helpful to your campaign?

Make a list of all your definite allies, as well as potential ones who might be persuaded to join you. (Start by googling "[name of your issue] + [your location]" to find institutions or influential people already working on your cause or similar issue.) Has a reporter two towns over covered another school's discriminatory dress code? Put her name on the list. Did a YouTuber just post a video about sexism at school? Add her too. Try to think locally as well as nationally and even globally. You're just brainstorming, so the sky's the limit!

Teamwork!

All the stuff up to this point is totally doable by you, along with just a couple friends. But a group effort can definitely make these tasks a lot easier, so now's a good time to start thinking about building a **campaign team**, a core group or squad who will literally be by your side when it comes to choosing tactics and executing your plan. It can be made up of friends or family members, you could enlist a favorite teacher or mentor, or you might put out a call on social media to widen your net. Remember, lots of important ground-breaking movements began with a handful of people with a shared goal or a unique idea who simply gathered around a kitchen table and talked about changing their world. Or the twenty-first-century version of that: a bunch of people chatting in a group message.

KNOWING YOUR ENEMIES

OK, "enemy" is a strong word, but let's be real—if you're passionate about doing something and someone else is passionate about stopping it? You are definitely not friends. The advice "Keep your friends close and your enemies closer" is pretty accurate in activism. In order to have a real picture of what you're up against, it's important to know *who* is up against *you*. So ask yourself

Who do I think will be openly hostile to my position?

Who is doing activism work that runs counter to my own?

Next, go online and research what these opposing groups or people are saying and doing. Find out who their leaders are and what they want to achieve. Determine what tactics they use. Then make a list of definite opponents and potential opponents.

The point of this exercise isn't to make a list of your mortal nemeses or even to come up with a way to destroy your adversaries. (I mean, unless that's your plan.) It's to take all this info into consideration as you decide on the most effective strategies and tactics.

Also, your enemies list isn't necessarily your targets list. In fact, the two should hardly overlap. Just because someone in power isn't currently supporting your cause doesn't mean you can't persuade them to—that's kinda the whole goal of activism. Rather, enemies are people or organizations who have about as much power as you do—meaning that they're trying to influence the same targets as you are—but they're entrenched in the opposite view.

KNOWING YOUR ALLIES AND OPPONENTS IS EXTREMELY HELPFUL WHEN MAKING YOUR PLANS.

They're your opponents in the zero-sum game: for one of you to win, the other has to lose. (Yes, in your ideal vision, they'll see the light and join your side, but for now, train your focus on the neutral targets.)

Let's say you want to organize a rally in support of overturning a law that discriminates against LGBTQ+ people. Are there groups or individuals who might be allies and willing to co-sponsor or speak or bring people in or co-organize—say, an equal rights club at your school? What opposition people or groups might hold a counter rally or use other tactics to work against yours? How do they try to win over public sympathy, and what can you do to help make your rally more attention grabbing and sympathetic to the public, either by beating them at their own tactics or counteracting them with your strategies?

Putting It All Together: The Power Map

Once you've determined your targets, allies, and opposition, you can create a **power map** to use as a visual for, well, mapping out what you're up against. Understanding who has the power to give you what you want (targets), who is on your side (allies), who can help connect you to your targets (secondary targets), and who is against you (opposition) will guide your decisions about the best tactics for your campaign—and a power map can help you get there.

On the chart below, write in all the people and organizations you listed, according to their structural power and whether they're for or against your cause. This isn't scientific, so just write each name where you think it fits best.

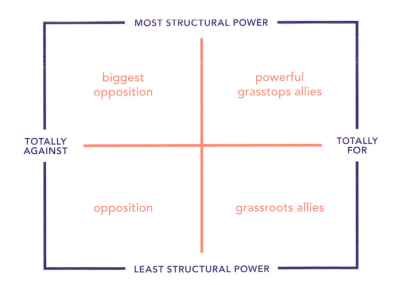

MOST STRUCTURAL POWER

biggest
opposition

powerful
grasstops allies

TOTALLY
AGAINST

TOTALLY
FOR

opposition

grassroots allies

LEAST STRUCTURAL POWER

When you've filled everything in, the people at the very top of the map will be your targets (or secondary targets), because they have the most power. The people to the right side of the map are your allies, and the ones in the top right corner are your most powerful, or grasstops, allies. (Grasstops advocacy is about mobilizing people at the top, those who already have influence and systemic power—get it?) The ones on the bottom right are your potential grassroots allies that, once organized, can help make a big noise about your cause. The people on the left are your opposition, with those in the top left box your biggest opponents.

Seem confusing? Try thinking about a power map outside of an activism context: Imagine you want to attend a concert in a nearby city, but your parents aren't sure they want to let you go. In this case, your targets are your parents—they have the most power to get you what you want, but they're not totally in support of you. They're at the top of the power map, somewhere in the middle.

Let's also say that your older sister is on your side—she's an ally to your cause. Your parents usually listen to her, so write her near the top and on the right of the chart. Another ally is your best friend, but she doesn't have much sway with your parents, so she goes on the bottom right side. Your brother, however, is against you. He goes on the upper left side.

Once you've mapped out your target and your allies, you can come up with an action plan. Maybe you can ask your sister (an influencer) to campaign your parents (targets) on your behalf or to offer to attend the concert with you. That's power-mapping in action!

Alone we can do so little; together we can do so much.

HELEN KELLER, American writer and activist

Resources

Now that you know what you want to do (your goal) and who can make it happen (your target), you're ready to take stock of . . . all the other stuff. Ask yourself:

What resources do I need to achieve my campaign goals?

What resources do I already have?

Your resources can be literal stuff like office supplies, a computer, or a phone app. They can be your friends who will volunteer, a teacher or advisor who can help you navigate any over-18 logistics, or your family who'll have your back. Other resources might be a popular social media account where you post, a meeting space you have permission to use, or money. Write it all down.

At this point, you probably don't know exactly how you're going to achieve your goals—and that's okay! (We'll get to tactics in the next chapter, I promise.) Creating a list of resources before you pick tactics can make your life a whole lot easier. For example, if you know you can reserve community space at your church, one of your tactics might be a fundraiser (since, hey, free party room!). Or if you have access to graphic design software at your school, you'll have an easy time making flyers, posters, or signs.

A list can also help identify resources you hope to get. Maybe you have a great idea for a block party to raise money for a women's shelter, but your resources don't include funds for snacks, supplies, etc. You'll want to revise your short-term or medium-term goals to include getting donations from local businesses or asking parents and friends to contribute space and supplies.

Planning so much before jumping into tactics can be boring or feel like homework. I get it—it isn't flashy or exciting, and sometimes it involves making lists. Ugh! But now we have so much more information (and we can do more than just running out into the streets and yelling at people to pay attention), you have a better idea of what you want to do. You might ask yourself:

- How will I grow grassroots power to have the most impact and influence over my target?

- How many people do I need to plan and staff an event? How many times will I host it? When?

- How many educational presentations will I give and to whom?

- How many petition signatures do I need to influence my target?

- How many times will I get the media to cover my story?

- When and how will I launch my shareable social media posts?

Tactics can include an infinite number of things or just a few specific things, such as petitions and letter-writing campaigns, meeting with elected officials, door-knocking, social media outreach, street theater, and lots more. We'll cover all these tactics and plenty of others in this book.

Now that you have an idea of how to build a plan, let's get into strategies and tactics and other stuff that will help you take the girl resistance to the next level!

✩ ✩ ✩ ✩ Takeaways ✩ ✩ ✩ ✩

1 Start with a plan that defines your vision and goals.

Real, lasting change takes forethought and strategy. Don't just scream in protest—get engaged for the long haul. Brainstorm and write down small, achievable objectives that will fuel your momentum and optimism.

2 Understand who your targets, allies, and enemies are.

You need to know who can make change happen, who's also fighting for that change, and who's actively working against it (and you). Do your research in this area. It will help make your goals more specific—and therefore more achievable.

3 Think hard about what resources you have on hand.

Then write down the resources your goals might require. If you don't have these resources yet, now's a good time to start thinking about how to get them. It'll be easier to pick tactics (in the next chapter!) that rely on what you already have or can easily get.

Protests, Petitions, AND Taking Action

"Take action!" is activist slang that gets thrown around *a lot*. You probably assume that taking action is what makes you an activist, right? Well, that's kinda true. But what action means can look a million different ways, from retweeting a post or making a donation to marching in the street, attending a meeting, or being the person who organizes that march or that meeting. So let's learn what to do to get things done.

LET'S DO SOMETHING! >

"I believe that telling our stories, first to ourselves and then to one another and the world, is a revolutionary act. It is an act that can be met with hostility, exclusion, and violence. It can also lead to love, understanding, transcendence, and community."

JANET MOCK, Black transgender author and activist, in *Redefining Realness*

When I was a kid, I watched my parents take action as members of their teachers' union. They planned fundraisers, drove around with protest signs in the trunk, and talked about union business over the dinner table. I learned from them that you have to fight for your rights and the rights of others.

The first time I participated in an activist action was in college, at a Take Back the Night march, which is a protest against sexual violence and domestic abuse against women. We walked around campus symbolically taking back the streets and chanting, "Yes means yes. No means no. Whatever I wear, wherever I go." This experience changed me fundamentally—as a woman, as an activist, as a survivor of sexual violence, and as a person. No matter which tactics you choose, you will remember that feeling of taking action: what community and solidarity and sisterhood and resistance feel like, in your bones, in your body, on your tongue.

In this chapter, we'll learn about several tactics activists use, the best ways to use each type, and how to use them in your own campaigns. Most likely, you'll use more than one tactic in your work. Many more exist than can fit in this book, but the strategies behind them all are similar.

How Do I Know Which Tactics to Use?

Before we explore the specific types of tactics, let's do a little more strategizing. First, review your campaign plan and remind yourself:

What is my goal?

Who are my targets, and how will I best reach them?

What strategies will achieve that goal and hold my targets accountable?

What are my resources, and what strategies can be done with them?

Your tactics should ideally line up with your strategies. You might use several of these strategies or focus on just one or two:

- **Building and recruiting:** getting people interested in your issue

- **Mobilizing:** getting your supporters to take action

- **Showing public support:** making it clear that a lot of people care about your issue

- **Showing power:** illustrating your power, in terms of either grasstops influencers or grassroots numbers

- **Educating the public:** helping people understand why your issue matters so they'll be on your side or take action

- **Putting pressure on a target:** directing your demands to a specific person or group

- **Attracting media attention:** reaching more people through media coverage of your issue

DON'T START WITH THE "WHAT"

Admittedly, this pre-planning stuff is not the most fun, and being strategic can be hard when you are *Just. So. Mad.* I often see new activists (of all ages) going right to picking a tactic before thinking about strategy—going to the "what" (usually a protest, the tactic most of us are familiar with) before the "why."

And that's not always a bad thing, especially when protests rise up in direct and immediate response to something egregious. Throughout history, protests that grew organically from the anger of the people being marginalized have helped spark national dialogues and long-term change movements.

However, just holding a protest is not the same thing as having an activist goal or a strategy. Without a **goal**, and a **strategy** to achieve that goal, a spontaneous protest can end up just being a one-off event. It'll feel good for riling up your activist spirit, but it might not change anything. (So if you haven't read Chapter 2 yet, you should check that out right now.)

Protests in and of themselves are rather ineffective at causing immediate change. A 2011 study by economists at Harvard University and Stockholm University found that a protest isn't what makes change; it's the action that happens afterwards. People who attend a protest are more likely to take action again after the demonstration, to engage in the political process, and ultimately to work as part

ALWAYS START WITH THE "WHY" AND THEN MATCH THE TACTIC TO THAT REASON.

of a campaign for change. But if you don't have a campaign, which is a productive way to channel all that energy that people bring to your protest, you'll hit a dead end.

Participating in my college's Take Back the Night protest changed me forever. Did it end rapes and rape culture on campus? No. Did rapists hear us chanting and change their ways? Unfortunately, not. Did it teach people about consent and how to make sure to have consent? No, again. Did it lead the campus administration to improve sexual assault policy at my campus? Nope. The march was mainly symbolic. The most impactful thing it did was to empower people to stand up and speak out about sexual assault.

So what does this mean for us organizers when we're choosing tactics? Always start with the "why" and then match the tactic to that reason. Make no mistake, a protest is a fine tactic, but it can't be your only tactic. Also think about how to move people to take action during and after the event, and which other tactics to combine with it to bring meaningful change.

Let's dig deeper into a bunch of activist tactics. We'll identify the forms each can take, the difficulty level, what it's awesome for, the time, people, and resources it requires, and tips for effectively using it in your work.

Taking It to the Streets: Demonstrations and Rallies

Demonstrations are public acts of protest meant to raise awareness and be seen by a lot of people. When most people think of taking action, this is what they think of: Marching in the street. Rallying in front of a government building. Chanting into a megaphone. Holding up signs and banners and fists in protest power. Demonstrations can take a lot of forms, not just marches and rallies, and can be pulled off successfully with small or large groups.

THIS TACTIC IS AWESOME FOR:

- Recruiting and mobilizing people to join your cause
- Showing public support for/against a person, issue, law, or cause
- Providing space for your community to gather and heal together
- Attracting media attention for an issue
- Publicly standing in solidarity with a larger campaign (like a national day of action)
- Disrupting the status quo in a small, specific instance

DIFFICULTY LEVEL: ●●●●●●○○○○

On a scale of 1 to 10, 10 being the most difficult, organizing a protest is a 6. Anyone can do it, truly, but it takes a good deal of coordination, time, and planning, and the larger the demonstration, the more difficult it becomes to pull off.

TACTIC TYPES

Rally: A protest in which large numbers of people gather to make a statement together, often accompanied by speeches and signs.

March: A moving protest consisting of a large gathering of people walking together on the sidewalk or in the street, often to a symbolic or high-traffic place.

Burma-Shave: A protest in which people stand on the side of a busy street holding signs that, together, spell out a message that people will read as they drive or walk by. (The weird name comes from an old-timey American brand of shaving cream that became famous for its unique advertising tactic of posting funny rhyming poems in sequential order on highway road signs.)

Guerrilla action: Any unconventional method of disrupting the status quo or promoting an activist message, such as:

- **Street theater:** An individual or group of people act out a dramatic scene or dramatic interpretation in a public place to make a statement.

- **Flash mob:** Many people meet in a public place at a designated time and perform a brief choreographed dance, song, or action and then quickly disperse.

Banner drop: Hanging or dropping a banner with your message from a prominent or symbolic location.

Civil disobedience: Actively and intentionally refusing to obey a law, command of government, or order from a person or institution in power. For example:

- **Sit-in:** Protestors sit in a symbolic or disruptive place until their demands are met.

- **Blockade:** Protestors block access to a building/place/street by standing or sitting in front of it and locking arms or chaining themselves to the doors/structure.

- **Walkout:** Protestors literally walk out of their school or workplace in an act of intentional resistance

Fill in the blank: There are many different ways to do a demonstration. The possibilities are limitless!

HOW MANY PEOPLE ARE NEEDED?

Varies. For rallies and marches, more is usually better! But smaller groups or even individuals can enact effective guerilla actions, street theater, or demonstrations with a visual impact *other* than a huge number of people. For example, a group of four can pull off an organized Burma-Shave on a busy street better than a rally, but a demonstration with 100 attendees is a great size for a rally, march, or flash mob.

TEAM ROLES

Ideally, you'll have people working with you when organizing an action. An organizing team may not be necessary for smaller demonstrations, but for a large rally, consider assigning specific roles, such as the following.

Decision maker(s)/lead organizer(s): makes big decisions and takes the lead role in organizing the demonstration

Peacekeepers: look-out for demonstrators, usually wearing arm-bands, a certain color of clothing, or another visible item that makes them stand out

Police liaison: coordinates communication between the organizers and law enforcement and communicates directly with police throughout the demonstration.

Emcees and speakers: speak during the demonstration (if there's an opportunity)

Media spokespersons: are prepared to speak to the media on behalf of the group/organizers

Accessibility monitor: ensures that the location and demonstration are accessible to all

Street medic: is on hand at the demonstration and equipped to provide immediate medical care if necessary

Street team: gets the word out about the demonstration

Videographer: records the demonstration

WHAT RESOURCES ARE NEEDED?

Signs and banners: Most demonstrations have some sort of visual element: signs, banners, T-shirts, costumes, props, whatever.

Megaphone or microphone: You may need sound amplification if you anticipate a large crowd or if someone will speak during the event. Try renting or borrowing a mic and megaphone from a local activist nonprofit, or buy one online. Find out if local laws require a permit for sound amplification. You can also use the People's Mic (see below).

The Human Microphone

The People's Mic is a way to amplify sound at a large demonstration without using equipment. First documented at anti-nuclear protests in the late 1990s, the technique was further popularized during Occupy Wall Street demonstrations in 2011 when protestors were denied permission to use sound devices. **Here's how to do it:** When someone wants to speak, they say "Mic check!" in a loud voice. Surrounding people loudly repeat "Mic check!" in unison. Then the speaker gives a message a few words at a time, and the people repeat the words in unison so that those who are farther away can hear.

Location: The location may be obvious, like outside city hall if you're targeting a local legislator. But if it's not, choose a place with high visibility, like a park or a busy street corner. Research local permits: you may be asked to pay permit fees, but if you can't afford them, ask for the fees to be waived. **No government can deny your permit solely because of an inability to pay.**

Social media: The fastest and easiest way to get the word out about a demonstration. Create an event page on Facebook or a moment on Twitter, and share a hashtag that protestors can use to show unity (and so you can find posts later).

HOW LONG DOES IT TAKE TO PLAN?

A demonstration in immediate response to an event can come together in mere hours, especially if coordinated by an experienced organizer. For example, in 2017 when U.S. president Donald Trump signed Executive Order 13769, commonly known as the first "Muslim ban," that would bar immigrants from seven specific Muslim countries from entering the U.S., thousands of people showed up at major airports mere hours later.

When a protest is planned in advance, it can take a few days or weeks or more to coordinate and spread the word—especially if the demonstration is large and lots of people are traveling to it. A large march in a major city organized by several people or groups in different locations would need to be planned months in advance.

5 TIPS FOR A DAMN GOOD DEMONSTRATION

1 **Think symbolically.** Demonstrations are symbolic. So is there a symbolic place or date that ties into your campaign? For example, you may remember the sea of bright-pink "pussy hats" worn by participants in the Women's March, a response to U.S. President Donald Trump's derogatory statements about sexually assaulting women. Or the "Hands Up Don't Shoot" chants and signs protesting the murder of 18-year-old Mike Brown by a Ferguson, Missouri, police officer during Black Lives Matter protests in 2014.

2 **Always center marginalized voices.** Are you rallying around an issue that directly affects you or your community? Or are you an ally, meaning the issue doesn't affect you directly but you support those who are impacted? If you're an ally, make sure to involve the marginalized people who are affected. Organize *with* them, rather than speaking around or over them, and align your tactics with what *they* want. Also, be sure your demonstration is

safe for marginalized people to participate in. For example, if you're protesting immigrants' rights, don't ask people to RSVP in a public way (like on Facebook).

3 **Learn about (and get) permits.** A permit isn't required for holding a demonstration on public property, such as on public sidewalks or in a public park. But having a permit can ensure that your protest can be held there or that counter-demonstrators (people protesting your protest—yeah, that's a thing!) don't have an equal right to be there. Unlawful arrests are also less likely at a permitted protest, which is important if participants are more likely to be targeted by police, like Black and brown people, trans people and gender nonconforming people, or immigrants. If you're marching in the street in the U.S., you'll need a permit to do it 100 percent lawfully because, although "the streets" are a traditional place for free speech, free speech can be restricted for safety reasons (for example, in most places it's illegal to block traffic).

4 **Amplify your voice on social media.** Protests and social media are about visibility, so use both to make this the loudest, most badass action it can be. Tell people about your demonstration ahead of time, but also show the power of your voices by going live during the action. Afterward, post pictures and videos. You could go viral!

5 **Know your rights.** This is maybe the most important tip of all. In the U.S., the right to protest is a fundamental freedom, but that doesn't mean it's never challenged. So before you plan or go to a protest, know what's legal and what's not. Educate yourself (visit the ACLU website) and ask local veteran activists for guidance. Know your rights in case of an encounter with the police, especially if you plan to break the law peacefully as an act of protest (see "civil disobedience," page 75). Have a plan in case you are arrested. And for *sure* share that info with trusted adults, such as your parents or guardians.

Power of the Petition: Postcards, Letters, and More

Petitioning, like protesting, is a bread-and-butter tactic of grass-roots organizing that has been around almost as long as the written word (so, like, almost forever). At its most basic, it involves getting a bunch of people to sign a document that affirms their belief in a statement and then delivering that signed document to the appropriate target to brandish some serious grassroots power.

You may have heard that signing petitions doesn't matter. This is totally false. Petitions can have a huge impact. Maybe one petition signature doesn't mean much (unless it's the signature of someone hugely influential), but lots of signatures do matter. The petition is a written equivalent of a huge protest—hundreds or thousands of people lined up behind a cause.

THIS TACTIC IS BEST FOR:

- Creating a visual representation of grassroots power
- Influencing a target to take a specific position, action, or vote
- Showing public support for/against a person, issue, law, or cause
- Raising awareness about your cause to a lot of people quickly
- Getting a political candidate officially on a ballot

DIFFICULTY LEVEL: ●●○○○○○○○○

It's inexpensive, effective, and totally super easy for anyone with basic writing skills.

TACTIC TYPES

Traditional paper petition: A sheet of paper with a few lines of text that clearly outline your demand to your target, often written as a letter: "Dear [TARGET], we urge you to vote for [THIS BILL] because [THIS IS WHY IT MATTERS]." Multiple lines for people to sign go underneath the demand.

Candidate petition: A document signed by a given number of registered voters to officially get a citizen on the ballot for political office. Each office has a different requirement for signatures that must be obtained before the potential candidate can file their paperwork. Since some signatures are bound to be invalid for one reason or another (signer isn't in the district or not a registered voter), you should aim for anywhere from 20 percent to 50 percent higher than the bare minimum.

Postcard-writing campaign: Not the vacation kind! This tactic consists of sending a huge number of postcards with messages that make the case for a particular change you want to see happen. Print your demand on postcards, along with the target's address, and ask people to sign and mail them. Works well because of volume: 100 signatures on a traditional petition is just a few pieces of paper, but a stack of 100 postcards is more impressive—or, okay, *annoying*. (Never underestimate the power of benignly inconveniencing someone to get their attention.)

Letter-writing campaign: Same idea as a postcard petition—a bunch of letters sent to a target making a demand—but with a bit more effort. You can print form letters to make it easy to get lots of signatures, but personal, heartfelt letters are more likely to be read by your target. Provide your letter-writers with powerful message points to use or be inspired by, as well as background information about the issue so they feel informed. Like postcards, letters also have an excellent visual impact.

Email and online petitions: These might be petitions for people to "sign" their names online or a form website that allows people to send individual emails with talking points directly to targets. Change.org is a popular site for setting these up, but you can also make a simple petition using Google Forms.

Social media petitions: Sometimes called a Twitterstorm or Twitter rally. Using social media to focus on an issue and tag a target is another way to show petition power. Apps like Thunderclap can help you coordinate a huge number of people to tweet on the same day and at the same time to create the biggest impact.

HOW MANY PEOPLE ARE NEEDED?

Creating an email or online petition can be done by one person. When it comes to canvassing the streets with petitions or postcards and clipboards, a small team is helpful: the goal is maximum number of signatures, after all, so having more people out at once (or in different locations) is helpful.

TEAM ROLES

You don't need a whole bunch of people to launch a petition collection, but you could divvy up responsibilities based on tasks:

Writer: drafts the demand portion of the petition that states the problem and the clear, concise demand of the target.

Collector: gathers signed petitions to prepare them for delivery to the target, especially if a whole bunch of folks are out collecting signatures.

Decision maker(s)/lead organizer(s): organizes the petitions, sorts them by address if necessary (for targeting elected officials), and strategizes how to deliver them to the target in the most impactful way.

WHAT RESOURCES ARE NEEDED?

Access to a printer or copier: For paper petitions, you'll need access to a printer or copier or modest funds for a printing service. If you're working with a nonprofit organization, they may be willing to donate printing costs. Most office supply stores, as well as libraries, have high-capacity copiers that you can pay to use.

Basic office supplies: pens for signing petitions and maybe a clipboard to hold copies.

HOW LONG DOES IT TAKE TO PLAN?

You can launch a petition in a matter of hours, even minutes. What takes time is all the stuff that comes *before*. Like deciding who the target is and which strategy uses petitions most effectively.

5 TIPS FOR A DAMN GOOD PETITION

1 **Collect contact info.** At a minimum make sure your petition has a space for people to write their address including ZIP code so that you can sort the petitions by legislative district (if your target is an elected official) and they can receive a response from the target. You can also include spaces for signers' emails and phone numbers and a checkbox for opting in to receive more info about your work. Then the petition doubles as a recruitment tool for volunteers and activists for your campaign!

2 **Play the numbers game.** The name of the game with petitions is getting lots of signatures, but "lots" can be relative: for example, 100 handwritten letters may be just as effective as 1,000 email petition signatures because handwritten letters are personal and require more time to write. Similarly, consider sending letters to a legislator's local, in-district office instead of their office in the state or federal capital. Local offices typically have smaller staffs and receive less correspondence, so 100 postcards may be a much bigger deal at the local office than in the capitol.

3 **Focus on influential signatures.** To give the collective voice of a petition maximum power, get a list of signers to whom the target must—or should—listen. For example, if your target is your senator, the signatures that matter most are of people who live in their district, who may (or may not) vote for them in the next election. If your target is a local bakery that's refusing to sell cakes to same-sex couples, aim for regular customers whose much-desired dollars will evaporate if the business doesn't change its discriminatory practices.

4 **Perfect your elevator speech.** We'll talk more about this in Chapter 4, but you want to be able to state the "what" and "why" of your campaign super-duper fast, especially if you're petitioning door-to-door or engaging people on the sidewalk. You've got just a few seconds to capture their attention and make your ask.

5 **Make it social.** Collecting petitions doesn't have to be boring or tiring. Have fun by hitting a busy public area with your friends. Go during a festival or public event, ideally one with lots of yummy food and entertainment. Host a letter-writing party with snacks and supplies.

Call for Justice:
Phonebanking Campaigns

You already know that your phone is not just a phone. On any given day, mine is a photo album, diary, to-do list, newspaper, mailbox, gaming device, bank, TV, and personal DJ. But a phone can also be a super powerful tool for social justice.

Phonebanking is kind of like petitioning, in that it's a grassroots tactic for reaching and mobilizing a large number of people quickly. In this case, a bunch of volunteers make a bunch of phone calls. Sometimes they ask people to call targets directly, but phonebanking is also a good fundraising or awareness-spreading technique.

THIS TACTIC IS BEST FOR:

- Mobilizing people to take immediate action

- Fundraising for your cause or for your campaign

- Influencing a target to take a specific position, action, or vote

- Showing public support for/against a person, issue, law, or cause

- Raising awareness about your cause to a lot of people quickly

DIFFICULTY LEVEL: ● ● ● ● ○ ○ ○ ○ ○ ○

In terms of logistical difficulty, phonebanking is pretty easy, though leading a phone bank takes planning and active volunteer recruitment. If you're phone-shy, this tactic can bump up to a 6 or 7.

TACTIC TYPES

Call-in campaign: Like a petition but conducted over the phone. The goal is to generate lots of contact with a target's office. Mobilize a group to call your target on the same day (or whatever makes sense) and flood them.

Fundraising phonebank: Calls for money. Whether you need donations to fund a particular tactic, or getting donations is your whole activist plan, phonebanking is one way to hit up potential supporters.

Polling phonebank: Those polls on the news that say "64% of [FILL IN THE BLANK] support [FILL IN THE BLANK]" are usually done via phone. Conduct your own survey by calling people with questions to learn more about how best to reach people with your campaign or how people feel about your issue.

Get Out the Vote: This method is used during political campaigns to remind people to vote and help them plan how they'll get to the polls. It's like a cheerleading call for voters ("You can do this! Here's how!"). You can volunteer for GOTV calls at any campaign headquarters on election day or join other nonpartisan, nonelectoral groups who do GOTV based on issues or upholding voting rights.

HOW MANY PEOPLE ARE NEEDED?

As many as you can manage. More people = more calls in less time. You can absolutely do a phonebank on your own but if your goal is to make a lot of calls, you'll want to recruit volunteers (or pick a different tactic that works for a smaller group).

TEAM ROLES

Decision maker(s)/lead organizer(s): makes call lists, recruits and manages volunteers, measures the success rate at the end of the action.

Phonebank volunteer(s): step up to phonebank with you.

WHAT RESOURCES ARE NEEDED?

Phones: I know it seems obvious but, like, you need some phones. An office that has multiple phone lines is great. If you're at someone's home, at school, or anywhere that doesn't have multiple phone lines, you can ask people if they're comfortable using their own cell phones. Alternatively, you can buy "burner phones," aka pay-by-the-minute cell phones aka super-spy phones, and loan them to volunteers for the phonebank period.

Meeting place: Ask a local organization to donate space, invite callers to your home, or meet in a quiet community space like a meeting room at a library.

Call list: Who ya gonna call? You'll need to source a list of phone numbers before you start dialing. Major activist campaigns may buy lists of phone numbers or go through the Board of Elections and compile a list of registered voters' numbers. You can get creative: try getting contacts from a school directory, the local phonebook, and an existing organizational membership or volunteer list. Alternatively, use email or social media to recruit callers for a call-in day, with participants calling folks within their own social networks.

Call script: Write a script for volunteers to read so they know exactly what to say and what to ask. Make copies for everyone to refer to during the phonebank. Lots of people get nervous talking on the phone, and a script can help them call with confidence.

CALL SCRIPTS

Your call script should be easy to read and say aloud. Include a place for the caller's name, especially if they're calling an elected official's office. Note that scripts are useful for tons of situations, not just phonebanks. Anytime volunteers are talking to the public about your issue, a script can help them feel comfortable delivering your message. Here are two samples:

Sample Script 1:

"Hi. My name is __FULL NAME__ and I'm a constituent of __TARGET__ . I live in __TOWN/CITY__ from zip code __YOUR ZIP CODE__ . I'm calling to ask __TARGET__ to vote for __BILL NAME (OR WHATEVER YOUR ASK IS)__ because __WHY IT'S IMPORTANT__ ."

Sample Script 2:

"Hi. My name is __FIRST NAME__ and I'm volunteering with __CAMPAIGN__ because __WHY IT MATTERS__ . I'm calling to ask for a few minutes of your time to __MAKE THE ASK__ . Can I count on you to __DO THE ASK__ ?"

A good call script includes three things:

1. The caller's name
2. The caller's relationship to the target (address and zip code for elected officials; that they are a student at your school if the target is your school board, etc.)
3. The issue the caller is calling in support of or against, stated clearly

HOW LONG DOES IT TAKE TO PLAN?

Running a phonebank requires minimal prep, but recruiting volunteers, finding space, and securing phones can take a few days or more. If those are locked into place—say, your friends are coming over to your place with their phones (check, check, and check)—then you're looking at a time commitment of either an evening (weeknight) or a late morning through early afternoon (weekend).

5 TIPS FOR A DAMN GOOD PHONEBANK

1 **Set realistic goals.** The reality is that a lot of your calls will be unanswered. That can be hard to slog through. Some people will think you're a telemarketer and may be rude and hang up. It's not personal! To motivate callers, set a team goal for successful calls (7 successful calls per hour per person is a pretty good rate). Have some sort of celebratory ritual, like a bell to ring, when someone makes a successful call.

2 **Pick the right time.** Phonebanking in the middle of a weekday while many people are at school or work is usually ineffective. The best times are Monday through Thursday in the evening. Avoid calling before 10 a.m., during typical hours of work or worship, or when a big sports game is on (seriously—people get mad!).

3 **Get creative with call lists.** If you don't have a full-on spreadsheet of phone numbers, ask each volunteer to call 5 friends and relatives. Or have everyone grab their phones, head to a busy area, and do a call-in campaign in real time, phonebanking on the spot!

4 **Keep good records.** Distribute a **call disposition sheet** (aka reporting form) to callers. The easiest way is to print a different section of your call list for each caller, with space to jot down the outcome. Some commonly used codes and abbreviations are:

- **LM:** left message on voicemail

- **NH:** not home, no answer

- **CB:** call back

- **WN:** wrong number

- **YES:** if they took action

- **NO:** if they refused or hung up

5 <u>**Make it fun.**</u> Meet up with volunteers a little earlier than official calling time to get them excited and give tips for successful calling. (Food helps!) We all know that phone calls can be awkward, especially when calling strangers, so making the phonebank social will help your team feel more comfortable and encouraged. And more likely to come back next time!

Resist Dot Com
Digital Organizing

In Chapter 1 we talked about the cartoons, TV shows, movies, music, and other media content that sexualizes, shames, and stereotypes women and girls. By creating empowering digital content—*by* girls and *for* girls—we can take back the narrative of our experiences and identities.

Digital organizing is a growing field that focuses on getting people to take action online to bring about real-life change. It includes developing apps or websites, hosting hack-a-thons, and making and sharing social media content, videos, blogs, online petitions, and the like. It doesn't have to be separate from boots-on-the-ground organizing. You can have a campaign or activist project IRL and create a digital component for it, like a Twitter rally or online petition.

THIS TACTIC IS BEST FOR:

- Educating people on your issue and the change it needs
- Influencing a target to take a position, action, or vote
- Showing support for/against a person, issue, law, or cause
- Recruiting and mobilizing people to join your cause
- Fundraising for your cause or campaign
- Getting media attention for an issue
- Publicly standing in solidarity with a larger campaign
- Raising awareness about your cause quickly

DIFFICULTY LEVEL: VARIES

But if you're pretty good with apps and tech (like if you have a smartphone and know how to work it), you're looking at an average level of 2 out of 10.

TACTIC TYPES

Texting: Sending text messages with a call to action for recipients to attend a meeting, call a senator, sign an online petition, share something on social media, or other was to support your issue. Hit up a list of volunteers or like-minded personal contacts.

Twitter rally: Like an IRL rally (see page 73), but online. Gather with others at a specific time on Twitter, using a hashtag specific to your Twitter rally. Ask people to "attend" by following the hashtag and retweeting the tweets. Getting big names to participate as "speakers" during the rally is ideal. Like in an IRL rally, have an ask for "attendees" to take action, such as tweeting at an elected official, signing a petition, or committing to volunteer.

Email list: Create a list of people who signed up to volunteer or be contacted about your campaign. Email updates as well as calls to action. You can do a mass email (be sure to bcc to keep everyone's info private!) or use a mailing list service like MailChimp or Constant Contact.

Facebook events or page: A good way to connect with supporters in a place tons of people visit every day. Make sure to invite your friends and ask others to do the same. The 2017 Women's March started with a simple Facebook event!

Photo petition action: Volunteers and supporters share pictures of themselves doing something symbolic or holding a sign with a message and hashtag. (Bonus points for tagging your campaign targets.)

HOW MANY PEOPLE ARE NEEDED?

Lots of people are needed to take action, but only a few to do the work of organizing. Once it's online, it can grow *fast*.

TEAM ROLES FOR DIGITAL ORGANIZING

Decision maker(s)/lead organizer(s): organizes the digital strategy

Data master: keeps track of all the data coming in, from people's contact info to participation analytics for your photo petition to how many people took action on your Facebook page. That info can then be used to mobilize interested folks for calls to action later.

Content creator: updates your digital presence or creates unique shareable content for your campaign. A great role for a friend with tech or design skills!

WHAT RESOURCES ARE NEEDED?

Internet access: As of 2015, almost half of the world has access to the internet, and the vast majority of young people have access at home or through their cell phone. If you are not among them, seek out libraries and internet cafés.

Basic graphic design software: Not necessary for all types of digital campaigns, but helpful if you want to whip up Twitter headers, shareable images, Snapchat filters, what have you. Use the software that came with your computer or websites like Pixlr or Canva (both of which have mobile apps, too).

HOW LONG DOES IT TAKE TO PLAN?

Not very. Like most things in social media, digital organizing tends to move quickly. Hashtag today, gone tomorrow, if you know what I mean.

5 TIPS FOR DAMN EFFECTIVE DIGITAL ORGANIZING

1 **Create original content:** Don't just recycle material from other sources—make something unique and shareable especially for your campaign. Visual branding is even more powerful than words (because honestly, who doesn't scroll past those walls of text?). If you have access to a smartphone or a tablet, you have a video camera. If you have an Instagram account, you have a pretty decent photo editor. If you use Snapchat, you can create and purchase a custom geofilter for your next activist event.

2 **Use your network:** Don't be afraid to ask friends and family to share your digital content, even if they don't have a huge personal social media presence. The more your content is shared and engaged with, the higher it tends to rank in all the fancy secret algorithms, and the more people are likely to see it!

3 **Reference pop culture:** Digital organizing is one part of activism where you can get silly with your message. Don't be afraid of punny hashtags or funny gifs. The more clever and relatable you are, the more people will be into your message.

4 **Win the internet with storytelling.** If funny and silly isn't your style, the other way to win hearts and minds is with a poignant and honest story. If you feel safe doing so, share with the world why your cause matters to you personally.

5 **Let haters hate:** With the internet come the internet trolls and, frankly, you've just gotta ignore them. Do not engage: block, hide, or mute them. If you feel threatened in any way, take action: document harassment (e.g., take screenshots of abusive tweets), report inappropriate activity to the social media network, and tell an adult. Most empty threats are just that but you should never feel like you have to tolerate someone making specific, targeted, violent statements at you.

Girl Activists Today, Voters Tomorrow:
—— Lobbying Elected Officials ——

If you're younger than 18 in the U.S., you can't legally vote yet. But that doesn't mean lawmakers don't pass laws that affect you, or that the people in elected office aren't interested in what you have to say! You have the constitutional right to take your concerns to your government leaders, the same as anyone else, regardless of whether you're able to vote.

Some people think that elected officials don't care about young people, that they want to hear only from voters, or big donors, or experts. That's completely untrue. In my experience, teens sometimes get listened to *more* than adults. Teens speak up because they care deeply about their communities, and legislators know that. The most powerful lobby visits I've known have been with young people who were honest and smart and unafraid to speak the truth.

Now, truly more than ever, girls need to feel empowered to speak up for their rights. We're under attack in so many ways. If we don't speak for ourselves, who will?

THIS TACTIC IS BEST FOR:

- Empowering people to speak up for their rights
- Influencing a target to take a specific position or make a certain vote on a legislative issue
- Influencing a target to make a public statement of support for (or disavowal of) an event, cause, or group
- Showing public support for/against a person, issue, law, or cause

---

DIFFICULTY LEVEL: ●●●●●●●○○○

I'm going to level with you: This one's tough. Not because talking to legislators is hard, but it requires basic knowledge of the political process, which can seem like an incomprehensible mystery. In addition, it often centers on a specific bill, law, or policy, which may be challenging to understand. That said, if you're working with an experienced activist, group, or organization, they can help break down the process and make the law or issue clear and simple for you. In which case this tactic is like a 3 out of 10—super doable.

Who Represents You?

No, really. Do you know who represents you? It's okay if you don't, and it's totally easy to find out.

★ Your **local government** is probably run by a village board or city council or something like that, with the mayor or town supervisor serving as the head executive. You probably also have a governing body at the county level with a legislature and county executive.

★ Your **state legislature**, which deals with state laws, is made of two houses, similar to Congress, with the governor holding the executive seat.

★ Your **federal government** is governed by Congress, made up of as the House of Representatives and the Senate, with the president in the executive seat.

Want to know who, specifically, represents you? Go to the League of Women Voters website (lwv.org) and enter your zip code to find out.

TACTIC TYPES

Different kinds of lobby visits serve different goals. Mainly, a lobby visit is an opportunity for you to work with an elected official on an issue (or get them to discuss it) *or* it's a power play, where you show them how much support exists for your issue.

Power lobby meeting: A sit-down with the legislator and celebrities, CEOs, or other rockstars, or with a big group of grassroots volunteers. I've been in lobby visits with more than 50 people. The purpose of a visit like that is to flex muscle, whether from social status or sheer numbers, and visually demonstrate how much support your bill or issue has.

Closed-door meeting: A smaller, more private visit with just a few people and the legislator. The goal is to have an in-depth conversation and hopefully get the official to agree to your ask. It's about building toward your campaign goals, not about a show of force.

In-district visit: A visit at the hometown office of a state or federal legislator. Members of Congress have an office in the U.S. Capitol and at least one office in a district region (a Congressional district for a representative, or the whole state for a senator). The benefit is that you don't have to go to Washington, D.C., so you're more likely to convince other local supporters to join you.

Drop-by visit: An unscheduled visit, when you just pop by an office, usually with a topic in mind and a leave-behind (see page 100), as well as your business card or a signature in their guestbook. Rarely will you actually catch the representative, and you may not even be able to talk to their staff if everyone is super-busy. A leave-behind helps them remember that you came.

Bird-dogging: the fine (and slightly obnoxious) art of following your legislator around to their speaking engagements and activities and speaking up about your issue or asking questions. You just show up and ask the tough questions. One of the goals of bird-dogging is to show elected officials that the public cares about their issue and to put them on the spot in front of other people—and possibly the media—when they don't necessarily have their perfectly polished talking points at hand.

HOW MANY PEOPLE DO YOU NEED?

You could go alone or bring a huge group. It depends what you want to accomplish, what your existing relationship is with the elected official, and how many people you can realistically mobilize.

TEAM ROLES FOR LOBBYING

Lobby team leader: The leader kicks off the meeting, sets the tone for the meeting, and introduces attendees to the legislator. They also keep the meeting on track by introducing other speakers and answering questions from the legislator to the best of their ability.

Note taker: Conversation can fly fast in a lobby meeting. It's always helpful to have someone take notes to share with the group later about what was said, what was asked of the legislator, what questions the legislator or the lobby group had that were unanswered, and the overall outcome of the meeting.

Storyteller: If possible, lobby visits should include people directly impacted by the policy or law who can share their personal story.

Data driver: A member of the group (or multiple members) who picks a few specific points, statistics, or messages and makes sure that they're the focus of the meeting. They can work closely with the leader to keep the discussion from getting derailed and ensure that questions are being met with meaningful answers.

WHAT RESOURCES WILL YOU NEED?

Research: If you're visiting to discuss a written bill, policy, or piece of legislation, be ready to present the issue clearly. It's entirely possible your lawmaker knows absolutely nothing about it, even if they should. Take this as an opportunity to be an expert! Do your research, and bring notes.

Leave-behind: Printed material that's, well, left behind. A leave-behind can be a simple one-page summary of your cause, a fully designed brochure, or a signed letter outlining your issue. This is a good way to ensure your issue is remembered after you leave or if you are unable to meet.

Thank-you notes: After the visit, send a thank-you note to the legislator to remind them again about you and what you discussed.

HOW LONG DOES IT TAKE TO PLAN?

If you know your issue well, planning won't take that long—it will involve gathering data for your research, articulating your cause, and organizing volunteers (and coordinating rides). The limiting factor here is your legislator's schedule: you'll have to call, write, or email their office, request a meeting, and then . . . wait. Local visits with federal officials may be contingent on when they're "home" instead of in Washington. Some are booked weeks in advance (or claim to be, anyway). You may have to submit a formal written request or speak with their scheduler. So play the long game, and don't give up: as a citizen, this kind of meeting is your right.

5 TIPS FOR A DAMN GOOD LOBBY VISIT

1 **Get a little personal.** While researching, look at your representative's voting record on other issues (find voting records on the U.S. Senate website, county/city websites for local politicians, or by simply googling their name and an issue) or at public perception of their interests and performance. This is to determine how likely they are to support you.

Learn more about the representative personally, too: Look up what civic groups they are involved in, what their former and/or current jobs are outside of holding public office, what types of issues they typically back. Maybe you'll find you have a hobby in common or you both go to the same religious house of worship. Do they do a lot of work on children's issues? Try to relate your issue to youth issues. Were they a Girl Scout? So are you! How can you tie the values of the Girl Scouts into your visit?

> **THE MORE YOU KNOW ABOUT THE PERSON YOU'RE MEETING, THE BETTER YOU CAN TAILOR YOUR MESSAGING TO THEM SPECIFICALLY.**

2 **Always end with an ask.** Every lobby visit needs an ask of the elected official, a clear action for them to take. A common ask is for an elected official to support or oppose a bill or policy, but you may have other asks, such as denouncing a local hate group, issuing a statement on a recent tragedy, or even publicly supporting your organization (hey, invite them to a fundraiser or rally—why not?). Don't leave a meeting without trying to get an answer—yes or no— or at least a plan for follow-up.

3 **Stay on message.** You want to invest some serious planning time on your messaging. What do you want to say and how will it help you work up to your ask? Can you use facts, logic, compelling stories, and other devices to drive your points home? How are you going to convince your representative to care about what you're saying? The better you know your messages, the less likely you'll get tricked into going off-message, which is (unfortunately) a tactic legislators use when they don't want to answer your ask.

4 **Play defense like a pro.** Think about how you're going to answer difficult questions or bust myths about your bill or topic, and practice responses ahead of time. Who is your opposition in this case and what are they saying? Can you refute their arguments or respond directly and proactively to the false information they're spreading? If you go in prepared, you won't get caught off guard.

5 **"We are the ones we have been waiting for."** This quote, attributed to Black bisexual anti-war and civil rights activist June Jordan, sums up the whole reason that girls are shaping the future. Quite literally, you will be voting really soon! And you'd best believe that elected officials know that. In 2018, the millennial generation will officially pass the baby boomers in the number of eligible voters. We're the most racially diverse generation and we're progressive, on social values and in general. Whether elected officials are ready or not, young voters and soon-to-be voters will be shaping the future, and you're going to shake things up. I know it! In the meantime, get involved however you can: volunteer on a candidate's campaign, plan a lobby visit, and help lead the even-younger generation of voters and future voters in the resistance.

☆ ☆ ☆ ☆ *Takeaways* ☆ ☆ ☆ ☆

1 You need to know why you're pursuing a cause before you decide what you're going to do about it.

Think of examples of spontaneous (or planned) protests that ultimately led to no measurable change. What could the organizers have done differently to ensure a greater level of success? Now think of successful demonstrations. How and why did those strategies result in progress and change?

2 Consider the complexity and human resources needed for the tactics you'd like to pursue.

Demonstrations, rallies, and protests need a lot of people to organize and execute. Petitions, letter-writing campaigns, digital awareness campaigns, and lobbying officials can be done by a smaller group of people.

3 Get comfortable speaking up.

Public speaking isn't always easy—and it's not for everyone. Figure our your strengths and weaknesses. If you feel you can't address a crowd or even a small group, it's okay to call on an ally to help you. But try to gain confidence—you're awesome and you can probably do it with practice!

☆ ☆ ☆ ☆ ☆ ☆ ☆ ☆ ☆ ☆ ☆

Messaging, Media,

AND

Mobilizing

When it comes to activism, words aren't just words. Words can tell stories and change perspectives. Words can slash down bigots and trolls. Words can get policies changed and laws passed. Words can turn people's hearts and minds. *Your* words are powerful. They can create messages that resonate with other girls, bringing us together in sisterhood. When girls' voices are silenced, when people speak over you or ask you to be quiet, they're trying to take away your power. Don't let that happen!

LET'S SPEAK UP! >

"When we speak, we are afraid our words will not be heard or welcomed. But when we are silent, we are still afraid. So it is better to speak."

AUDRE LORDE, writer and activist

Are you sometimes so angry or sad or upset that you can't find the words to express how you feel? When I feel like I've lost my words, I think of Audre Lorde. She was a Caribbean American, Black, lesbian poet, scholar, and activist with a powerful voice. She spoke out about issues of race, gender, and class, focusing on creating space and uplifting power for Black women.

Audre Lorde had her first poem published when she was fifteen years old. It was a love poem titled "Spring." In a 1991 interview, she said, "I was one of the editors of our high-school magazine and wrote a love sonnet for the magazine. But a teacher said . . . it couldn't be published. So I submitted it to *Seventeen* magazine and it was published there." Take that, teacher!

So far we've been exploring how to take action and plan, how to *do* stuff. Now let's figure out how to say stuff. We'll learn to craft messages that show what you're doing and why it matters. And all with your very own words!

What Is "Messaging"?

Messaging is everything you put out to the public that tells what your campaign is about. It's a strategy that takes your campaign plan—your goals, targets, potential allies and opponents—and distills it into words that resonate, persuade, and cut to the heart of your issue. It's about using your words to win.

You already know about messaging—we all look at advertisements our whole lives. Have you noticed that the best messages are often the simplest? But don't be fooled—that doesn't mean they're simple to create. A good message strategy will answer the four Ws:

Who is your group/campaign/organization?

What is the issue or problem?

Why should people care?

What must we do to solve it?

An effective message will "hook" your audience—grab their attention and keep it. A good hook (or what some in media call a "peg") is something you can metaphorically hang your story on: an image, event, or phrase that's timely, persuasive, and compelling. When coming up with your hook, ask yourself:

- Why is my issue important *right this very moment*?

- What about it is something people will feel a personal connection to?

- How can I tell the story in a way that makes people feel stuff?

(((The Three Types of Messaging)))

Good messaging doesn't hit people over the head with all the info all at once. When it comes to making long-term change, being loud and pompous might get attention, but it won't motivate people to get up and *do* anything. What will? Below are three key types of effective messaging, which we'll explore in this chapter. You can use all three in one message, or a combination, or just one at a time. You don't need three different messages. You just need to know that messages can have different purposes.

1 Awareness If people aren't aware that your issue is, well, an *issue,* they won't know why they should care about it. And they definitely won't do anything about it. Awareness messaging is the first thing that most people will see or hear about your campaign, so it's gotta be attention-grabbing. Don't get lost in the details. Focus on big, public, easy-to-understand, catchy messages.

2 Persuasion Now that people know what your issue is about, you've got to explain why it's so important and convince them to join your side. Here's where you get into the specifics, share personal stories and hard facts, and point people toward forming an educated opinion. Ultimately, your goal is probably to urge people to do something: volunteering with your campaign, signing a petition, protesting, etc. Persuasion is all about providing the necessary info so that people feel personally invested, fired up, and willing to act.

3 Mobilization This is the call to action. The big ask. It's where you tell people exactly what you want them to do, when, and how. And, most important, to inspire them to hit the pavements and fight alongside you.

AWARENESS MESSAGING

Sometimes you need to be brief and bold and get right to the point. Raising awareness is about quickly showing people that an issue or cause exists, not giving them a long explanation. It's about capturing people's focus so you can move into the more persuasive part of your message. The first step is answering those "Wait, who are you?" and "What's going on?" questions that people will inevitably ask.

The Name Game

Coming up with the perfect name for your group or campaign or team is part of your messaging plan. Why? Because your name is key to sparking awareness of your cause. Names communicate the *identity* of your group as much as they do the *facts* of your mission. So if you pick a name that's hard to understand, confusing, or way too long to remember, then it's (a) not going to make a great first impression and (b) not going to help you build awareness and credibility for your cause.

It's usually not a great idea to come up with a name by yourself—you can't think of everything and might miss a subtle meaning or fail to highlight the most important aspect of your cause. Try a group brainstorm. Bounce around ideas with your team or, if you're working solo, run it by family or friends. Start with a brain dump—list all the words, phrases, and ideas that you associate with your campaign. Look at your campaign plan and think about your goals, targets, and strategies. What word(s) will help you meet those goals, reach those targets, and execute those strategies?

Force Kindness Shelter Justice Action Zero Tolerance Equality Empowerment

Every campaign or organization name should be:

- **Simple** Your name shouldn't be super hard to say, so use words that are easy to spell and read.

- **Easy to Remember** A name doesn't have to be punchy, catchy, or cutesy, but it should be something people won't forget. Alliteration and rhyming are good techniques, and short names are always better than long ones.

- **Representative of Your Core Values** Your name is an opportunity to frame your cause with *feelings*. You don't have to be dry to sound "official"—it's okay to throw in words like *friendship*, *caring*, *empowering*, or other emotion words to make your cause seem human.

- **Acronym Friendly** If your name is more than one word, you'll likely start referring to it by its initials or as an acronym or nickname. Consider how pronounceable that is (and make sure it doesn't spell anything unintentionally funny (like B.U.T.T.).

A great example is Planned Parenthood, the United States' oldest and largest provider of reproductive health services, including abortion, birth control, and cancer screenings. Everyone knows what Planned Parenthood is about and remembers its name. It's short, easy to say and understand, and memorable thanks to alliteration. It also speaks to the organization's core values. PP's mission is to provide services and healthcare, but its ultimate goal is to enable people to make empowered and informed decisions about pregnancy and parenting, thus its name.

Here's a personal example: Some friends and I wanted to create an unbiased talkline for women who have had abortions, providing safe space for them to talk openly with a supportive person. We

were inspired by a similar organization in California called Exhale. We spent several long meetings and all-day brainstorming sessions before we settled on Connect & Breathe. It was easy to say, easily abbreviated (C&B), catchy and inviting, and it emphasizes our focus on support through listening. It's much better than End Abortion

THE NAME OF YOUR GROUP OR CAMPAIGN IS PART OF YOUR AWARENESS MESSAGING.

Stigma, which is a good slogan but not a good name. Connect & Breathe is also discreet, so people would feel comfortable displaying our info in waiting rooms and doctors' offices.

Sometimes, though, it might make more sense to be specific and direct. A group I helped found decided to call ourselves the Coalition for Police Reform. The name is clear and to the point, and it has a catchy abbreviation, CPR. Perhaps most important, it's easy to figure out what our issue is and what we're trying to accomplish.

Your name is what the media will focus on if they cover your work, and it's how you'll introduce your work to others. Coming up with a really good name isn't as important as what you do, but it sure does help increase awareness of your cause!

Catchy Slogans

Marketing companies are all about slick jingles and trendy taglines. Corporations spend billions to develop messages that stick in customers' minds: *I'm lovin' it. Think different. Because you're worth it.* But don't worry—you can craft your own unforgettable activist slogans that capture the attention of the media, potential supporters, and your targets, all without spending a dime.

In marketing, there's a theory about "five touches" (or three touches or eight—there's a bunch of versions of this idea; the exact number is kind of whatever). The basic concept is that the average person needs to be exposed to a message five times before they're fully aware of what it is (or that it exists at all).

You've definitely seen this marketing technique in action, even if you didn't realize it until now. Let's say a company is releasing a new soda flavor. They'll push out an ad campaign that engages potential buyers several different ways. You, the target of the ad, will:

- Catch a funny commercial during your fave show (1st touch),

- Watch a video ad on your phone while googling (2nd touch),

- Scroll by a sponsored ad on your Instagram feed (3rd touch)

- See a banner ad on your favorite blog (4th touch).

All this will happen at roughly the same time. Then, in a store, you'll see a special display for the new flavor (5th touch) and think, "Oh yeah. I've heard this drink is good" and, hopefully (for the soda company), buy one. That's how the five touch strategy works. Sneaky, huh?

Activist slogans can work in a similar way. They won't be the entirety of your messaging plan, but slogans do help people become aware of your issue and remember it when they hear it again. So how to come up with a slogan? Well, as Nike says, *just do it*. (See?!) But seriously, an **effective slogan** is:

Short   Five or six words max. You can expand on your issue in the persuasion stage of your messaging.

Catchy   Easy to read, understand, and remember.

Specific   Avoids generalities, vague terms, or specialized language.

Impactful   Evokes emotion and sparks action. It's OK to be dramatic!

Two additional slogan hacks:

- When you come up with a slogan, ask yourself, **would this make a good chant?** Say it out loud. The slogan doesn't have to be the same as your chants, but a good chant is easy to say aloud and has a natural rhythm. Your slogan should have these qualities too.

- Then ask yourself, **would this make a good hashtag?** It doesn't have to be your hashtag, but a good slogan is short and easy to read and catchy—just like a good hashtag.

Case Study:

No activist slogan has been more powerful in recent years than #BlackLivesMatter. It was created by three queer Black women: Alicia Garza, Patrisse Cullors, and Opal Tometi. They describe #BlackLives Matter as "a movement, not a moment," meaning that it's more than just one protest or single issue. It's about building lasting change and demanding the rights and dignity of all Black people.

#BlackLivesMatter is a literal hashtag. It's a chant heard at rallies across the country. It's a national organization with chapters all over the United States. It's a brilliant slogan that's sparked action across the world, captured the attention of the media and elected officials, and changed the landscape of resistance to police brutality and the murder of Black people.

Wait, But How??

Activist causes aren't always easy to understand. Maybe it's a complex policy issue, or it involves lots of terms the average person has never heard of, or maybe people just plain don't know about stuff.

Several years ago, when I was working on organizing support for the Affordable Care Act, I couldn't get people to understand what the bill *was*, let alone how it would help them. The healthcare marketplace was complicated and confusing, and, on top of that, the bill was being called four things: the Patient Protection and Affordable Care Act (actual name), the Affordable Care Act (shortened version), the ACA (acronym for shortened version), and Obamacare (nickname). A lot of the work was just making sure everyone was on the same page about the name—then explaining what the ACA would do and why it was a good thing.

YOUR JOB IS TO MAKE YOUR MESSAGE SHORT, SWEET, AND SIMPLE.

In any issue campaign, you'll have to break down your big ideas into educational sound bites that people can grasp and retain. It might seem counterintuitive—big, scientific-y terms sound really impressive, don't they? But the reason they're impressive is that people don't really know what they mean.

Here's how to make sure as many of your targets and audience get what it is you're talking about.

Don't agonize, organize.

FLORYNCE KENNEDY, African American lawyer and activist

Define terms If you're using acronyms or lingo that is specific to your issue or cause, make sure you're defining those terms as you're using them. "Hi, we're trying to expand access to LARC methods of birth control at the health center. LARCs, or long-range acting reversible contraceptives, are safe and reversible birth control methods that stay effective for years and are proven to be the most effective at preventing unplanned pregnancy."

Use plain language This isn't the time to break out your SAT vocab or legal jargon or techy terms. Speak about your issue in a way that's easy to follow. People will more likely relate to what you're saying and be persuaded to take action. "I'm here to talk about making our city a sanctuary city, a place where immigrants are welcome and able to live their lives free from the fear that local police will turn them over to federal authorities."

Use analogies, metaphors, or examples Explaining an issue in concrete language helps ground complicated, abstract ideas in reality. "Anti-discrimination laws will *break down the barriers* that prevent LGBT people from being safe at work in our state and *shine a light* on the need for LGBT-friendly workplace policies."

PERSUASION MESSAGING

This second stage of your messaging is persuasion: People know *what* your thing is, now they need to know *why* it matters. As you're educating people about concepts or terminology in plain words, you can set the stage for persuasive messaging. Tactics like using stories and statistics help put the complex issue into a more relatable and personal context. This is where your listeners are gonna want details, statistics, facts—basically, proof. You don't have to whip out a PowerPoint pres, but definitely be prepared.

Talking Points

If you'll be speaking at a rally or talking to a target or writing a petition or doing anything, you need to write down a few talking points. These are the mini messages and super-strong statements that you want to make sure you don't forget.

Why should you do this? Well, have you ever gotten into a big screaming fight with your bestie or your parent or whomever? (Of course you have.) You might say something you don't really mean, or try to make a point but epically fail, because you're so frustrated you can't get the words out of your dang mouth.

That's because you were being *reactive*—you were responding to what the other person was saying instead of saying what *you* wanted to say. When you're being reactive you're following, not leading the conversation (or screaming sesh). Talking points flip the dynamic so that you know what you want to say before the other person says anything. They allow you to stay in control of the dialogue. That's how you persuade someone!

Talking points also keep you from rambling, veering off topic, or losing track of your goal when speaking about your issue. This comes in handy if a reporter tries to get you to slip up and say something controversial, or a legislator tries to get you off topic to avoid answering your questions, or an opponent tries to push your buttons in order to win a debate.

The key to making super-persuasive talking points is to brainstorm messages in advance. I like to bring in a saying from my college creative writing classes: "Show, don't tell." In creative writing, that means helping the reader *experience* the story, not just *describing* it to them. It's fine to tell someone why something is important, but that won't engage them. When you *show* why something is important, it sparks people's imaginations and analytical skills and leads them to draw their own conclusion. Look at the two examples on the next page.

TELL   vs.   SHOW

"Hi. Will you sign this petition about reproductive rights? It's super important!"

"Hi. Would you sign this petition to make sure the government doesn't take away our birth control? Birth control is basic preventative care that 99% of American women use at some point in their lives. Can you take just a minute to sign this petition to save birth control?"

"I urge the school board to adopt a policy to support and protect transgender and gender nonbinary students at our school. It's the right thing to do."

"I urge the school board to adopt a policy to support and protect transgender and gender nonbinary students at our school. According to the Gay Lesbian Straight Education Network, 75% of transgender youths report feeling unsafe at school, had significantly lower GPAs than cisgender classmates, and were more likely to miss school because of concern for their safety. You must act not only because it's the right thing to do, but because trans students deserve equal access to education."

See the difference between "telling" and "showing"? *Showing* someone the facts lets them make up their own mind—hopefully by agreeing with you. *Telling* is just you ordering them to think the way you do, which doesn't work unless you have mind-control superpowers.

So how do you "show" that an issue is important? Through a multi-pronged but very doable approach:

Topline Messages   What are the two or three mini messages you want people to hear? Keep them short and simple. Use plain language, and make each message its own separate point.

Facts & Logic   What numbers and statistics back up your position? Facts establish credibility for your claims and show that your messages are rooted in logic and the truth. That said, facts alone can be boring and they don't make people "feel" why something is important. Facts need to be paired with values to get the most bang for your messaging buck.

Values   What are the core values of your campaign and how do they align with values that most people hold? In messaging, values are positive and empowering, and because they tend to be universal, they're a good way to help convince someone to get on board with your cause. Examples of values are freedom, justice, fairness, integrity, happiness, honesty, and equality. Mention how one (or several) are involved.

Stories   Think about the last heartbreaking viral video you watched. Most likely it was focused on people or animals and what happened to them. Stories bring emotional impact into your message and promote empathy and action for your cause. How does your issue/problem affect real people? What have they been through? What's your story, if you're directly involved? How would success in your campaign affect people by making their lives better?

Message Triangles

This tool comes from the business world. Message triangles are meant to be used in the "art of persuasion" for salespeople and public speakers and the like. They're useful for organizers and activists too because we're also selling something: not nail wraps or leggings, but the motivation to sympathize with our cause, meet our demands, and take action NOW.

Why a triangle? Because most people can memorize three messages before their brain is overloaded, so it's a strategic way to get in as much info as possible before overwhelming your audience. You can jump between any of the talking points at any time, which is especially helpful when giving a speech or media interview because that's more like how we naturally talk.

The message triangle works like this: Your primary message goes in the center of the triangle, with your three different topline messages on each side. Topline messages should be brief—one sentence written in plain words. Write supporting facts, stories, examples, and messages under each topline message.

I prefer message triangles to lists because lists can make it seem like the points have to go in a certain order or that the ones at the top are most important. But that's not really how talking points are meant to be used. (Imagine reading someone a list! They'd zone out for sure.) Unlike a list, a triangle has three equal sides that are all connected. Use one to practice talking about your issue.

MOBILIZATION MESSAGING

Once you've made people aware of something and convinced them it's really important, now it's time to mobilize—a.k.a. get them to do whatever it is you need them to do to move closer to your goals.

Call to Action

It doesn't matter how fired up and educated someone is about an issue: if they don't know what they can do about it, they probably won't try to find out. Your final job as organizer is to make it as simple as possible for your supporters to take the rage and passion that your awareness and persuasion messaging have stirred up and channel them into a specific, concrete action.

Ever read an article about something really horrific and feel like, "That sucks. I wish I could do something." It's *dis*empowering to feel you don't know what to do to make change. People want a call to action. So giving them something to do, even if it's small, can be really empowering and good for them. And obviously it can help you build grassroots power too.

As with slogans and message triangles, the call-to-action tactic comes from the business world. You encounter these marketing messages all the time. Every time you see an ad that encourages you to "Sign up for free" or "Join our email list" or "Shop now," that's a call to action. The difference, again, is that we're selling social justice. The call-to-action part is the ask, the direct prompt for someone to do something. Here are some good concise examples:

- Call your legislator about a bill or policy
- Retweet or share a message on social media
- Sign a petition
- Join as a volunteer
- Sign up for an email list
- Come to an event

Your call to action should be direct, specific, short, yet comprehensive. If it's too long ("Join our cause by supporting girls and making your voice heard when you give your time to sign this petition . . ."), you may lose people's interest entirely. Include everything the person needs to do immediately (e.g., a call script and phone number if the call to action is to make a phone call; the info to join the event; a contact form to sign up as a volunteer). It helps to say how much time it will take: "Do you have just two minutes to share this on Instagram and Twitter?" Seriously, who doesn't have two minutes?

It also helps if you link back to your awareness and persuasion messaging, to show why the call to action is so urgent right now this very minute!

Here's an example of how it can all come together:

Condom availability programs, school programs that provide free or low-cost condoms to teens *(awareness)*, have been around for a long time *(awareness)* and are super effective at reducing unintended pregnancies and STIs *(persuasion)*. The majority of teens say they face real barriers to accessing condoms and studies show teens are more likely to stay safe if they have free, confidential sexual health services including access to contraceptives *(persuasion)*. Can you take a minute right now to sign this online petition to the school board asking them to vote "Yes" on the condom availability program? *(mobilization)*

Social Pressure

This is a nice way of saying "peer pressure"—but good peer pressure. Not like pressuring a classmate to skip class. Unless you're planning a walk-out protest action, in which case, maybe it's pressuring a classmate to skip class.

Social-pressure tactics involve tapping into people's FOMO. Yes, guilting or tricking people into doing the right thing (but again, not in a mean/bad way). Several studies have shown that social pressure works really well in getting people out to vote. A 2010 study by researchers at the University of California and Facebook found that showing Facebook users a message with pictures of their friends who voted was more effective than a message with just voting information in getting people to vote IRL. Seeing your friends doing something gives you a sense of FOMO that makes you want to join in the "I Voted" sticker selfie party!

Another way to motivate people to take action is to use guilt and accountability, which sounds harsh, but I swear it's not evil. A study on voting by the American Political Science Association found that people were more likely to turn up to the polls if they received a mailer threatening to share with neighbors their voting history (not who they voted for, just whether or not they voted at all). I wouldn't suggest threatening your neighbors, but this kind of social pressure can work to mobilize people: "Everyone is coming to the rally tonight! Will you be there too?" is more effective than "Not a lot of people said they can come, so we need you to show!" (Who wants to go to a party with no one there, right?)

Social pressure works offline too. Has your school ever organized a Prom Promise campaign, encouraging students to sign a pledge saying they won't use drugs and alcohol at prom or won't drive drunk after prom? That's a social pressure campaign. Can you get people to sign pledge cards to take an activist action or go with you on a lobby visit or join your campaign team?

Media Outreach Basics

Now that you've developed each type of messaging for your campaign, it's time to get the word out. A **media strategy** is a really good addition to your campaign plan. Why? Because the media have the power to reach a ton of people and drive them to your cause.

The term "media" used to mean newspapers, magazines, and TV programs. Today it's a gigantic world of blogs and digital magazines and video and social media. But getting someone to pay attention to your issue and your work hasn't really changed—it's just on a much bigger and faster scale. A Facebook Live video can go viral in an instant. Mainstream news outlets often comb social media looking for stories. Something that happens at a rural high school can become national news overnight.

Even better—*you* can be a creator of these stories in ways you never could before. Are you on Facebook or Tumblr or Twitter or Instagram? You're probably already a media-content producer!

EFFECTIVELY COMMUNICATING WITH THE MEDIA IS KEY TO A SUCCESSFUL CAMPAIGN.

While planning your campaign, think about the role media can play. If you're holding a press conference, don't choose a time when members of media are less likely to come, like a weekend or late at night. Make sure you get the word out to reporters and focus on coming up with a good hook to attract their attention. Most important, think about the media as another tool to move your targets.

Each of the three types of media described on the next pages can generate a "hit," which is a public relations term designating every mention of your brand that appears in the media. In this case, the "brand" is you and your activist work.

▶ **Earned Media** Any media that cover your story for free, including blogs, newspapers, TV and radio stations, and that shares and retweets on social media. You *earned* this media at no cost to you. Most of the time, earned media is what people mean when they say "the media."

■ **Owned Media** Any media that you *created*, including your own social media presence, graphics or videos you made, your website, your blog.

● **Placed Media** Any media that you bought, like ads, paid promotions, blog content you paid someone to write or post.

Let's go in depth to better understand how to work with these media types during your campaign.

▶ Earn It!

There are tons of ways to get media to pay attention to you, but first let's think about your campaign goals and what kinds of media strategies will get you where you want to be.

SEND A PRESS RELEASE OR ADVISORY

A **press release** is an announcement of something you think is newsworthy that goes directly to media outlets. It can be up to two pages long and describes what the newsworthy thing is and why it's important. See the sample on the opposite page for tips.

An **advisory** is an invitation to attend an event or press conference; it's usually short, just the important info. These traditional ways to reach out to media are changing, however. Email is the best for sending these, although simply messaging or tagging reporters and writers active on social media can be equally effective.

SAMPLE PRESS RELEASE

A press release always has four components: a strong headline, contact info, an informative and compelling opening paragraph, and a couple brief paragraphs that tell the story of your announcement. Here's an example.

FOR IMMEDIATE RELEASE
Media Contact: Your Name
555-555-5555
you@girlsresist.com

The Girl Resistance Marches in D.C. to Demand Rights on the Day of the Girl

WASHINGTON, D.C., October 10, 2018 — Thousands of girls from all over the nation will convene on the National Mall on October 11 at 12:00 PM to commemorate the Day of the Girl and to demand equitable rights for all. This convening will be the largest youth-focused march in U.S. history, completely organized and led by girl activists.

The Day of the Girl is an international celebration created by the United Nations in 2012. On this Day of the Girl, girl activists will come together to show the power of the girl resistance and to demand a better future for girls and all young people. March organizing team member [Your Name] says the Day of the Girl March is about "showing that girls are strong, smart, and powerful and that we aren't going to settle for less than full equality for all people here in the U.S. and all around the world."

SUBMIT TO EDITORS

Pretty much all newspapers have an editorial or opinion section. News articles are supposed to be unbiased (even if they don't always come off that way), but the *editorial page* is the one section where the papers' editors can write their own opinion about a topic. It's also where they print opinion pieces from others and reader-submitted letters to the editor. Use all of these to your advantage!

Write an opinion piece, or **op-ed** (shorthand for "opposite the editorial page"), and submit it to a newspaper. Know how many opinion pieces your local paper gets from girls or teens? Not very many. According to the OpEd Project, the writers are "mostly western, white, older, privileged and overwhelmingly (85%) male." Your voice would definitely stand out, especially if you know what you're talking about. And you do! You totally do!

Remember your message points, your facts and logic and values and stories? Those are perfect for opinion pieces, which are all about persuasion messages with a bit of awareness messaging through in. And because the whole point is to express your viewpoint, you can focus on exactly what you want to say.

Sending a brief **letter to the editor** can also get your cause or campaign into a print or digital media outlet. These usually have a word limit, as well as other guidelines for publication, so go to the website of your chosen paper(s) or magazine(s) and follow the directions. Letters are most interesting when they reply directly to something the paper already published or when they come from local readers, so try to peg your opinion to a topic recently reported on.

Lastly, if you think your topic is really newsworthy, you can **pitch** it directly to the editorial team. Much like a press release, you send info about your campaign to the head of the editorial board and formally request an in-person meeting. Editorial board meetings typically work best if you have a really good hook and an issue with major local impact.

BLOGGERS AND INDIE MEDIA

These days, blogs have just as much influence as traditional news outlets, if not more. In short, blogs are legit.

Because they can update as often as they want, blogs may be more likely than major news outlets to pick up a seemingly random story (and major outlets often read blogs for trending stories), so getting your campaign covered by an online outlet can be really helpful. Pitch your story right to a blog or specific blogger. Do a Google search and comb through social media to see which bloggers are writing about issues similar to yours. Look for feminist blogs or girls' blogs or social justice blogs.

In your pitch or press release, ask them to cover your story. Send pictures. Offer to provide an interview for their audience. In many ways, getting your story on the *Huffington Post* may be more effective than getting it in your local paper, especially if your work is on a national scale or especially edgy and current. Pitching on the internet is quick and free—so do it as much as you want!

Blogs That Cover Activist News

- ★ Autostraddle
- ★ Bitch Media
- ★ Buzzfeed
- ★ Colorlines
- ★ Crunk Feminist Collective

- ★ Democracy Now!
- ★ Everyday Feminism
- ★ Feministing
- ★ Huffington Post
- ★ Independent Media Center

- ★ Mic
- ★ Upworthy
- ★ Rewire
- ★ Slate
- ★ The Root
- ★ Vox

INTERVIEW TIPS FOR MEDIA-SAVVY GIRLS

What if someone from the media actually takes you up on that interview or, even better, reaches out to you before you reach out to them? Great! Except now you have to do an interview! Eeek! Here are some tips for going "on the record" with a reporter, writer, or anyone else.

Always Comment Never say "No comment," like they do in the movies. If you do, you risk the reporter writing, "She refused to comment," which makes you sound all kinds of shady. However, you don't have to take every media request. You can politely decline by saying you're busy and unavailable or you can say if you don't feel like you're the appropriate person to comment.

Be Prepared If a reporter calls for an interview but you're not ready, ask to get back to them before their deadline. In the meantime, do you homework so you'll be ready to rock.

Use Your Message Triangle Put your thoughts in order before an unexpected interview.

Don't Be Caught Off Guard by Live Interviews Always ask if the interview is live. If it's held at a studio, arrive early so you have time to mentally prepare. If they're bringing the camera to you, find a place where you feel comfortable, ideally somewhere with a simple backdrop: your living room or dining room, or outside your home, or at an office.

Stick to Your Talking Points The interviewer may try to get you to answer controversial questions or catch you saying something incorrect. Practice and memorize your talking points, supporting facts, and messages. If you don't want to answer or are stumped, use a "bridging phrase" to bring things back to your topline messages (see below). It is absolutely acceptable to pause, redirect, or change the subject. Most important, never ever ever ever ever EVER lie!

Simple Bridging Phrases

"That's a good question, but the real issue is…"

"That's a common misunderstanding. In fact, …"

"The most important thing to remember is…"

"I think the big issue here is…"

"That reminds me…"

"I understand what you're saying, but…"

● Own It!

The best thing about owned media is that you completely control the messaging. It's DIY media and, although the goals are similar to working with traditional media, you have a lot more freedom.

Women and girls have a long history of creating our own media when no one else was covering our stories or hearing our voices. Back in 1848, a group of women organized the first women's rights convention in Seneca Falls, New York, where they drafted the Declaration of Sentiments, a manifesta for women's equality modeled on the U.S. Declaration of Independence. It was really kind of badass for its time, and you could argue it was the first widely circulated feminist document in America. In 1972, Gloria Steinem and a small group of women fed up with the patriarchy in media conceptualized, created, and printed the first issue of *Ms.* magazine—the first magazine created, written, and operated entirely by women.

Since then, literally thousands of women-created, DIY media outlets have popped up in print and online. Because the media world is still mostly dominated by men, women and other marginalized groups must create our own ways of sharing information and news with one another.

MESSAGING FOR SOCIAL AND DIGITAL MEDIA

Social media is one of the easiest ways to create owned media. A Facebook or Tumblr or even Pinterest post can go viral in minutes. Increase the odds by posting pics or graphics that link to your campaign. Other ways to build owned media, which can then be pushed out to generate earned media, include:

Create a Campaign Website Make a site for free on WordPress or Blogger or other user-friendly platform. Some companies (like Nationbuilder) host platforms specifically designed for activists

Riot Grrrls and Zines

Zines are short, usually handmade indie publications that are photocopied and distributed in small batches. Feminist activists and artists have been using zines to spread information, build awareness, and make change pretty much since the photocopier became a thing. In the 90s, the Riot Grrrl underground punk movement meshed feminist politics and punk politics through all-girl bands that directly confronted patriarchy in society and the male-dominated punk scene. Bands like Bikini Kill, Sleater-Kinney, and 7 Year Bitch inspired a music-focused feminist resistance in which women could scream and express themselves the same way men did. And they screamed about issues that matter to us, like sexual assault, violence against women, racism, sexism, homophobia, and sexuality.

Zines were common markers of the punk scene subculture and became a huge part of the riot grrrl scene. The word "grrrl," a growl-y spelling of "girl" meant to take back the word's power and express anger and strength, emerged from some of those early zines. Literally cut and pasted together, combining essays and artwork and collages and politics, zines shared info and built community, which is how they're still made and used by artists and young people today. Print zines have slowed a little because of the internet, but you could argue that Tumblr and Instagram and Snapchat are all digital zines, where girls create discourse and share art and information. The movement lives on!

and nonprofits, with built-in widgets for donations, petitions, and events, but may require a subscription fee.

Set Up Campaign-Specific Accounts Use the same name for each account for brand consistency. For example, if your Twitter handle is @girlsresistandpersist, your facebook URL should be facebook .com/girlsresistandpersist and your YouTube handle should be youtube.com/girlsresistandpersist.

Host a Podcast All you need is a decent microphone and some basic sound-editing software (like Apple's GarageBand).

Send an Email Newsletter It may be a bit old school, but collecting email addresses and sending updates on your cause to your supporters is a super-fast and simple way to share information and keep people up to date, especially as your campaign grows.

Start a Blog Who better to write about your campaign than you? Start a blog where you put your own spin on issues and promote your posts on social media and to other blogs and sites.

Use your knowledge of awareness, persuasion, and mobilization messaging to amp up your social and digital media outlets and create shareable content. Try tweets similar to the ones below that combine the messages you've learned about:

> Did you know that 3 out of 4 transgender students say they feel unsafe at school? It doesn't have to be that way! Click here to sign our petition to the school board to protect trans kids at our school! http:// yourlink.here (awareness, persuasion, mobilization with call to action)

> Trans and gender nonbinary students deserve to be safe at school. Do you agree? Join us at the school board meeting on Wednesday at 6pm. I'll be there and we really need you there, too! (persuasion, mobilization with a call to action and social pressure)

TIPS FOR AD DESIGN

What info is most important? For the ad copy (i.e., the text in the ad), avoid using a ton of words. Focus on your topline messages, your catchy slogans, your hook.

★ Make that the biggest text on the ad. Your eye should be drawn to it immediately.

Who's going to see it? Think about your audience and what info they'll need in order to understand or connect to your issue. What call to action does it make sense to ask of them?

What will it look like? A strong visual image can go a long way to creating an eye-catching visual, especially important given all of our screens both large and small. You can find lots of free clip art and stock photography online (look for royalty free and/or creative commons licensed images).

★ Use only images that you have the rights to! You can get in big trouble if your ad uses a pic or artwork that you don't own, so don't just yank something from Google Images.

★ Use high-res images (at least 150 dpi) for photos or pictures, especially if the ad is for print. If you don't, your pictures may look blurry and unprofessional.

What's missing? Make sure all pertinent info is there! Don't forget to include what the ad is for, how to take action and/or whom to contact, where and when the event is, etc. Double, and then triple, check that all info is correct before you send the ad to print or publication. You'll thank me later!

What email subject lines will get recipients to open your message instead of deleting it? Which of these would you most likely open?

Subject: Weekly Update on Trans Student Campaign

Subject: Protect Trans Students at Our School

Subject: We Need You Now! Trans Students Deserve Safe Schools.

You'd probably open the last, which uses more targeted mobilization messaging to convey urgency. Remember to message to win!

■ Place It!

Most grassroots campaigns lack the resources to place paid media. On a more affordable scale, however, you could buy a Facebook ad for 25 bucks to promote your campaign page or an upcoming event locally. Or place a small ad in your local paper or magazine for a nominal fee.

Before creating your own ad, think of one you've seen recently.

Why do you remember that ad?

What made it stand out? A catchy slogan? A strong visual?

Did you see the ad in various places?

The ad is one of your five touches, so it should resemble your other messaging to ensure that people realize they're all for the same campaign. See the "Tips for Ad Design" on the previous page for the basics of creating a successful ad.

☆ ☆ ☆ ☆ Takeaways ☆ ☆ ☆ ☆

1 "Messaging" happens in three stages: awareness, persuasion, and mobilization.

How does the Never Again MSD gun-control organization, founded after the mass shooting at Stoneman Douglas High School in Parkland, Florida, succeed in its messaging? Why are its hashtags #NeverAgain and #EnoughIsEnough so powerful?

2 Telling people that your cause is important isn't as effective as helping your audience experience the story behind an issue and connect with it emotionally.

Spend an hour or two coming up with two to three talking points that make the case for your cause. Research facts to strengthen your argument, and be sure to know them when pressed to defend your position. "Knowing your lines" will help you master the art of public persuasion.

3 Communicaton is key.

How can you best use varied media to get your message out? Write down the advantages and disadvantages of tactics such as press releases, blog post, op-ed, or interview with a reporter. After evaluating your strengths and resources (including your time!), which ones will bring you the most success?

* * *

Fundraise

FOR THE Girl

Revolution

As you probably know, women's and girls' work has long been underpaid, whether it's our work in the home, in the office, or in the streets. From a young age, girls are taught to self-sacrifice and make space for others; we're discouraged from asking for what we want. Girls work for free, all the time. But we deserve to have our work recognized too. We have a right to ask for money for ourselves and our social justice work.

LET'S GET FUNDED! ›

"The most common way people give up their power is by thinking they don't have any."

ALICE WALKER, African American writer and activist

Having money often makes life easier. Basically, money is power—the power to buy a car so you don't have to take public transportation, the power to get an education, the power to make yourself feel good with self-care necessities. We live in a capitalist society, one in which money (getting it *and* spending it) is the be all and end all. It may feel impossible to do anything without money—especially once you've gotten into the thick of your campaign planning (T-shirts and posterboard don't grow on trees, after all).

But money isn't the most important thing when organizing for change. As we explored in Chapter 2, your resources extend way beyond dollars and cents. People have always done activist work without funding because resistance movements fight back out of necessity. And they're often led by those who are directly affected—the people who are marginalized and oppressed and, therefore, probably not very wealthy. The girl resistance does not *depend* on being funded by rich people. But we damn well *deserve* to be.

This chapter is all about how to get some of that much-needed cash to help you reach your activism goals. Just remember that it's a privilege to have enough money so that you don't need not think about the basics—food, housing, clothing—and still have some left over to put toward your activism.

How Much Money Do I Need?

Your activist work deserves to be funded, and you should not feel bad about asking for money to advance it. The two primary reasons you may need money for your activism are:

1 You're raising funds or collecting goods to donate directly to people who need support, meaning that your fundraising is the activism.

2 You're raising money to help pay for the costs of your campaign, meaning that your fundraising is to support your activism.

Before you start fundraising, think about what you need the money for.

Are you raising money to donate to a charity or cause?

Do you need money to travel to a big rally or training session?

Do you need to buy T-shirts or buttons or signs for an action?

Do you need to print flyers or handouts?

Do you need to rent event space or equipment?

It may sound like you need a lot of money, but you don't. Never let a lack of cash hold you back. There are free online petition sites, free email list-management software, free website hosting, free email programs, free document sharing sites, free social media access, and free event space. There's DIY alternatives to signs and T-shirts, and low rates for making copies at your local copy shop. You may be able to get services and goods like graphic design or T-shirts or event space donated.

Being a girl activist has always been about being resourceful. So whether your campaign budget is $50 or $50,000, now's the time to get out in the world and make some damn change.

The ideas in this chapter will help you build a framework for your "asks" (requests for money) so that you will feel confident and be successful. You will feel like a fundraising boss who totally knows what she's doing. (Because you are! And you do!)

MAKING A BUDGET

A budget is an estimate of income and expenses, which might sound complicated but it really isn't. You just need to know what's coming in (income) and what's going out (expenses). A budget breaks down expenses into individual items and allows you to determine what target sum will cover your costs but is still realistic and attainable.

A budget is a working document, meaning that it can be updated as your campaign changes—and it likely will. For example, let's say you were hoping to win a grant but didn't. You'll have to figure out new fundraising ideas for income, or reduce your expenses, to still hit your target.

So let's figure out how to do this important first step in fundraising. Grab your campaign plan and let's make a budget! (I promise, it's easier than you think!)

1 **Review the resource section of your campaign plan.** Where do you need resources you don't currently have? For example, event space, art materials, funding for transportation.

2 **Review the strategies and tactics in your campaign plan.** Go through them one by one and see what, if any, are the associated costs. For example, pizza for meetings or renting sound equipment for rallies or sign-making supplies for demonstrations. Imagine yourself executing the tactic step by step—what will you need?

3 **Estimate costs for each item.** If you don't know a fair estimate for something, research the average selling price. Think about how many times you might need that item. For example, if you need food for four meetings and you estimate food will cost $50 per meeting, you'll need $200 total (4 meetings x $50 = $200).

PRO TIP: *It's better to overestimate than underestimate. Budgets are aspirational. The goal of budgeting is to help you figure out what you'd ideally raise to fully fund your campaign.*

---

4 **Create a budget based on your estimated costs.** Use the template on the opposite page to write out a simple budget statement, or use a spreadsheets program like Excel or Google Sheets.

5 **Plan how to bring in income or donations to cover costs.** We'll get more into specific ways to do this later in the chapter. For now, just jot down your ideas.

6 **Calculate your overall profit or loss.** First add all your projected expenses and your projected income separately, and then subtract the expenses from the income. That number will be your net profit (or loss). "Net" in this case means the amount that remains after all charges and costs have been deducted.

7 **Adjust as needed.** Your aim in fundraising is not really to make a profit, like a business would, but you are trying to cover all your expenses. If your projected net income is higher than your projected net expenses, congratulations! Your accounts will be in the black, as they say (i.e., you don't owe anyone for anything and have money left over). But if the opposite is true, you'll be in the red and will need to lower your costs, raise more money, or do both to make up the difference. (See "Getting Out of the Red" on page 146.)

Sample Budget Template

This template is filled out as though the campaign is over and all your expenses and income have been reconciled, or checked against each other. Your "actual expense" and "actual income" columns will be blank when you first create a budget. You'll fill them in after your purchases and fundraiser are complete.

EXPENSES	PROJECTED EXPENSE	ACTUAL EXPENSE
Food for 8 meetings	$400	$500
Poster printing	$100	$50
Total Expenses	$500	$550

INCOME	PROJECTED INCOME	ACTUAL INCOME
Donation drive	$300	$400
Grant	$250	$250
Total Income	$550	$650

PROFIT-LOSS	PROJECTED	ACTUAL
Total Income	$550	$650
Total Expenses	$500	$550
Net Profit	$50	$100

KEEPING THE BOOKS

After you've created your budget, you'll want to keep track of your *actual* expenses and income. Bookkeeping is vital to a fundraising plan. It's helpful to you not only to stay organized but also to be able to show what you used the money for if donors or grantmakers ask.

As you hold fundraisers, solicit donations, and buy supplies, record *everything* you spend and *everything* you take in. Compare these numbers to your projected budget and ask yourself:

Am I hitting my targets?

Am I exceeding them?

The sooner you know which direction you're headed, the quicker you can correct your course.

Getting Out of the Red

What do you do if you end up in the red—aka don't have enough funds to cover your expenses? First off, don't panic—it's not the end of the world. There are a few ways to approach this problem.

★ You can slash your expenses and just not spend as much (maybe you won't be able to buy pizza for your meetings after all).

★ Or you can try to find someone to donate what you need instead of purchasing it with campaign funds. (Maybe local restaurants or a friend's parents would be willing to donate food for your meetings? Hey, it never hurts to ask!)

★ Or you can try to bring in more money.

★ Can you host another fundraiser (or up the ante on a current one) to secure the funds you need?

TIME VS. MONEY

If you're like me, you'd prefer to DIY whatever you need, whenever possible. Like, when it comes to making protest signs. If it's only a couple dozen signs, making them myself is affordable and doesn't take too much time. But if I need 200 signs, you bet I'm going to pay a company to print them. Why? Because making that many signs would take up a week or more! That's what's known as **opportunity cost**—the difference between paying someone to do something and the time it will take to do it yourself.

But just because a DIY is time-consuming doesn't mean you should always pay someone to do it. There are grassroots solutions to opportunity-cost problems. Let's say you can't get the money or a donation from a copy shop to print the signs. How about throwing a sign-making party? Invite a bunch of friends to make signs and ask them to bring their own art materials to share. It takes more planning than doing it yourself, but you'll produce more signs in a shorter time. And probably recruit people to your cause to boot!

> **BOTH MONEY AND TIME ARE VALUABLE, AND IT'S UP TO YOU TO BALANCE WHERE YOU'RE WILLING TO SPEND THEM BOTH.**

Getting and Storing Your Campaign Cash

If you're gonna be raising and spending money, then you gotta think about how to accept that money and where to keep it. Here are a few considerations to keep in mind.

Open a checking account. This is your best option if you can do it. Just know that most banks require minors (teens, aka you) to co-sign with a parent or guardian. If that person doesn't have a good credit score, you may not be able to apply for an account. So how do you work around that? Try one of the options below.

Ask your parent(s) or guardian(s) to allow you to use their bank account or to set up an account in their name for you to use. But lots of people don't have a bank account. What do you do then?

Run a cash-only campaign. Get a locked cash box or a money jar or dedicated envelope in which to store your funds. If people insist on writing a check, they can make it out to you personally and you can cash it at a bank. Many banks will cash checks in small amounts even if you don't have an account there. This option works fine for small fundraising efforts (i.e., less than $1,000), but if you anticipate raising larger sums, you'll need a more secure system.

Seek out a nonprofit to manage the funds for you. If you go this route, donations to your cause go to the nonprofit, and you pay your expenses through their finance system. People who want to write checks can do so to the nonprofit. This can be really helpful if you'll be dealing with large sums of money.

Form your own nonprofit! See the sidebar on the opposite page for a primer on this route.

WHAT IS A 501(C)(3) NONPROFIT?
(And Should I Set One Up?)

Nonprofits, called 501(c)(3) organizations, are exempt from paying federal taxes and can accept tax-deductible donations. (The name comes from the section of the U.S. tax code that applies here.) To qualify, your organization must provide a public benefit by furthering a cause that's "religious, charitable, scientific, literary or educational, testing for public safety, fostering national or international amateur sports competition, or preventing cruelty to children or animals." Forming a nonprofit involves incorporating your group with your state and filing legal paperwork with the U.S. Internal Revenue Service.

Beyond tax benefits, making your nonprofit a 501(c)(3) can also get you privileges like eligibility for nonprofit-only grants or discounts on bulk mail postage. But it also means you can't make a profit (duh) or get involved in political campaigns (i.e., no endorsing or donating money to candidates). And your information on tax and filing documents will be publicly accessible.

So: is it worth it? A 501(c)(3) designation gives your organization legitimacy and donors may contribute more if they know they can deduct their gift. But you'll also have to incorporate your group at the state level (so that the organization exists as a separate entity from you and the people in it), pay a filing fee to the IRS, and just generally fill out a lot of paperwork. If your costs are low, and most of your donations are under a few hundred dollars, the designation might be more hassle than it's worth. But if you're starting to take in some serious revenue, and want a lasting structure and accountability for your group, it's worth looking into. You can find state-by-state 501(c)(3) resources at grantspace.org.

WHAT ABOUT A DIGITAL PAYMENT OPTION?

Increasingly, people prefer to pay for things digitally (or they just plain don't carry cash), so if you figure out a way to accept payments quickly and easily, you'll open yourself up to a lot of new donors. Most payment apps will receive funds for you, but you need to have somewhere to transfer the monies if you want to withdraw them. For that, you typically need a bank account or a credit card to hold the money until you need to use it.

WHAT ABOUT TAX-DEDUCTIBLE DONATIONS?

Probably the most complex legal question you will be asked is whether donations or gifts to your activism cause are tax deductible. The short answer is, not unless you are working with a nonprofit that is able to accept such donations or are setting up your own.

If you're already partnering with a nonprofit organization, it's likely they're approved to accept tax-deductible donations. Ask the administration what their process is—they likely write receipts to the donors, who then present them when they file their taxes at the end of the year.

You might also consider forming your own nonprofit. Establishing a nonprofit is a complex undertaking that involves several must-follow steps, but it's not insurmountable. There are pros and cons that you will need to weigh. If your cause is small and the donations you're soliciting are too, it probably won't make a huge difference to donors if they can deduct their contributions from their income. But if you're dreaming big, it's best to educate yourself on what it takes to become your very own nonprofit organization. For more on starting a nonprofit, read "What Is a 501(c)(3) Nonprofit?" on the previous page.

Fundraising Ideas That Are Super Easy, Dirt Cheap, and (Almost) No Work

Now that you've done all your prep, it's time to get that cash! Fundraising doesn't have to be complicated, especially if you're raising a smaller amount (less than $1000, although some of these ideas work for raising big bucks, too). Here are a few simple yet effective ways to get you started.

FUN AND GAMES

TIME COMMITMENT: Low
PEOPLE NEEDED: 1 to 3
BEST FOR: Last-minute fundraising; fundraising goals of $100 or less

Games work especially well if you set up at a special event or in a heavily trafficked area (like at your school or place of worship). The key is to get a whole lot of people to play in exchange for a small donation. Tap into their competitive instincts, and their wallets will just naturally open.

★ Guessing Game

Fill a jar with candy or buttons or marbles or whatever small item you choose. Have a stash of small slips of paper nearby. Challenge people to guess how many items are in the jar and write their guess on the paper for a small donation ($1 per guess). Be sure they include their name and phone number (so you can contact the winner). Offer a prize to the winner, like $10 in cash or a gift card to a local coffee shop or restaurant.

Take this game to the next level by tailoring it to your campaign. If you're promoting age-appropriate, comprehensive sexuality education, put condoms in the jar. If you're raising money for an animal shelter, use dog biscuits. Obviously, you'll need to keep an eye on the jar, so either stick with it all day if it's in a public spot or leave it in a safe place (like the front desk of your school).

★ 50/50 Raffle

This one is so easy and so inexpensive! For a period of time (a few hours at an event, a week-long fundraiser, etc.), you sell raffle tickets for a price you've decided on. Offer discounts to encourage people to buy more tickets—for example, $1 for 1 ticket, $2 for 3 tickets, $5 for 10 tickets, and so on. The more tickets a person buys, the better their chances of winning. And the more tickets you sell, the more you get to keep! On each raffle ticket, the person fills in their name and phone number. After the time is elapsed, you draw the winner. That person receives 50 percent of the money you collected, and you keep the other 50 percent. Everyone wins! (Tip: Buy rolls of pre-printed tickets with numbers from a party store or online.)

★ Penny Wars

This competitive game takes very little planning (take note, procrastinators) and works best when you're fundraising at school or a place where it's easy to form teams. (You could do homeroom classes as teams, for example, or pit graduating classes against each other.) Take empty jars, one per team, and decorate them. (Cutting the tops off clean milk jugs or soda bottles works.) Place the jars in a prominent place. Teams compete by throwing their spare change into the jars over a decided-upon amount of time. The team that raises the most money wins a prize, like a gift card or a pizza party, and, of course, bragging rights. Boost the competitive spirit by counting the jars daily and ranking each team's progress on a chart that everyone can see.

SOCIAL FUNDRAISING

TIME COMMITMENT: Medium (maybe one or two weekend days)
PEOPLE NEEDED: 1 to 3
BEST FOR: Getting small one-time donations; fundraising goals of $1,000 or less

Social fundraising, or peer-to-peer fundraising, is really hot now that online crowdsourcing through sites like Kickstarter and Go-FundMe have become so popular. (For more on how to build a successful online crowdsourcing campaign, see page 157.) But even in the dark ages before the internet, activists hit up friends/family/distant acquaintances for donations and it worked like a charm. Here are some tried-and-true, old-school social fundraising ideas.

Ask your supporters, friends, and family to each write at least ten handwritten donation letters about your cause and send them to their personal contacts. Provide letter-writers with facts and messages about your cause and why it's important, which they can include in their letters. If you can afford it, include a stamped envelope addressed to you so that donors can easily get their donation into your hands.

★ Special Occasion

Instead of asking for gifts on your birthday or holiday, ask for donations to your cause. Try personalizing it for the occasion. For example, if your fifteenth birthday is on May 30, you could ask for $5 for the month of your birthday, $15 for your 15 years, or $30 for the date of your birthday. (Facebook makes this super easy with their new fundraising feature.)

★ Un-Event Event

Instead of planning a fundraising event, which takes time and work, send out invites to an "un-event" fundraiser—to *not* attend a party—and ask for donations instead. Make it a tea non-party and include a tea bag in the invite, or choose an inexpensive, easy-to-mail party favor that will amuse people and hopefully convince them to RSVP with a donation. Because, let's be honest, sometimes *not* leaving the house is more appealing than "actually going and doing a thing."

MAKE, DO, SELL

TIME COMMITMENT: Medium–high (a week or two for planning, a day for the actual sale)
PEOPLE NEEDED: 3 and up
BEST FOR: Working with a group; fundraising goals of $100 or less

Much like offline social fundraising ideas, selling stuff is a tried-and-true option that's affordable, simple, and fun. Just make sure your signage says what the money raised is going toward—you may just inspire people to donate even more if they're passionate about your cause too! If you have flyers or petitions, put those out as well.

★ **Bake Sale** Make some sugary stuff. Set up a table and a sign and sell your sugary stuff! DONE!

★ **Yard or Garage Sale** Ask friends and family and supporters to donate their gently used stuff so you can sell it for cold hard cash. Put up flyers in your neighborhood and post on online message boards to make sure all local bargain-hunters know to come—and be sure to mention it's for a good cause!

★ **Ribbon or Button Sale** Get buttons (either handmade or purchased in bulk from a local printer or online) or awareness ribbons (easy to make: cut ribbon, add safety pin, done) for your campaign. Sell them for $1 to $2.

★ **Car Wash** Set up at a local business, church, or organization—ideally near a high-traffic area like a grocery store or mall—that has a parking lot and easy access to water. You'll have to call for permission to use their property, of course; see if there's a parent or family friend who owns a business that you can approach. This is a great (and fun) option if you're working with a club or volunteer group on your campaign. Have one team hold signs by the road to lure in drivers while another team washes the cars and collects the cash.

★ **Pancakes, Spaghetti, or Ice Cream** Food is always a good bet for raising money, and this version makes it into the whole event. Find a space to host a meal (in a church basement, at an inexpensive lodge or hall, or in your home) and invite widely (be sure to ask for RSVPs so you know how much food to buy!). Ask for a donation of $5 to $10 per plate (make sure the attendance fee is enough to cover the cost of ingredients and make a profit) and prepare and serve the food yourself. A spaghetti dinner, pancake breakfast, or make-your-own sundae are popular and inexpensive options.

Startup Cash Flow 101

For many of these fundraisers, you'll need some money to get the stuff that your fundraiser needs to *make* money. So, how? For most, you need only $25 to $50 to start. Plus you can save money by using supplies you already have or borrowing from friends and neighbors. But where do you get that first $25?

★ Consider a short-term loan from your parents or supportive adults with a guarantee to pay them back.

★ Ask everyone on your campaign team to chip in $5 toward costs.

★ See if you can get your supplies donated by a business.

★ Break into your own piggy bank and pay yourself back once your fundraiser is up and running.

CROWDFUNDING YOUR CAMPAIGN

TIME COMMITMENT: Medium to high (a week or so to prepare the campaign, plus the duration of the campaign)
PEOPLE NEEDED: 2 and up (maybe 1 if you're really tech savvy)
BEST FOR: Small-medium one-time donations; fundraising across long distances; fundraising goals of $1,000 or more

Crowdfunding is a collective model for raising small amounts of money from lots of people through the wonder of the internet. A few popular sites are Indiegogo, GoFundMe, and CrowdRise. Then get to it!

★ **Create a page** Crowdfunding is an awesome opportunity to raise awareness about your cause (what with the internet being the easiest way to share literally anything). On your crowdfunding page, write about the ways people can support you *beyond* giving money, like volunteering or sending donations of goods or signing an online petition or joining your group. Even if people don't have the ability to donate, they will learn a little about what you're doing and may even choose to take action.

★ **Tell an Engaging Story** Use what you learned in Chapter 4 to show why donating to your cause is important. Personal stories and facts connect people with your cause and compel them to open their (virtual) wallets.

★ **Use Videos and Visuals** At a minimum, use a feature image or video, even if it's shot with your phone and just shows you talking about why your cause matters. A wall of text is dull and may make you seem unorganized to potential donors; pictures and graphs will make your point more quickly and entice people to keep reading. Shoot your video in the best possible lighting and make sure the sound quality is good (use an external microphone).

★ **Create Rewards for Donation Levels** Offering rewards encourages people to give a little more. The rewards don't have to be tangible or expensive. Offer a shout-out on social media, a hand-written thank-you note, short personalized video, or a Skype meeting. People like knowing that their donation is going to something specific and concrete, so break it down as much as you can. For example, if you're raising money for a local nonprofit that teaches English to immigrants, let people know that each $10 (or whatever amount) donation provides a new notebook for a student.

★ **Ask Friends and Followers First** Once you create an engaging fundraising page, it's time to put it out in the world. Asking for money may feel awkward, but remember—your cause deserves support! Send them a link to your page directly on social media. Email, text, or message them. If people can't give right now, ask them to share your call to action with their networks. Every share gets your message in front of more potential donors.

★ **Set a Stretch Goal** Don't sell yourself short with a goal that's too low. Determine a reasonable minimum amount to raise based on your budget; then, in the narrative of your campaign, add a stretch goal that's a bit higher. Sell people on what you'd do with that extra money. For example, if your campaign goal is $2,000 to buy 200 T-shirts, your stretch goal could be $2,500 to cover buying a button maker and supplies to make 500 buttons promoting your cause.

★ **Read the Fine Fine Print** Each crowdfunding site has different operating rules. Most will take a small portion of what you raise by charging fees for processing online donations and for their own costs of hosting your fundraiser on their site. Some sites only give you the money if you reach your goal. Some only fundraise for specific types of projects or causes. Most will release the money only if you have a verified checking account and identification (so this option may not work if you can't get or don't want a bank account). Understand what the fees and rules of the crowdfunding site are *before* you begin.

Forget Money...Get Stuff!

Money is great because it's flexible—it can be turned into anything, from boxes of supplies to professional services. But another way to think about fundraising is collecting what the professionals call "in-kind donations." That is, goods or services that aren't cash money. Maybe you have given to or helped organize a donation drive. That type of action is also part of fundraising even though you're collecting items, not money.

DONATION DRIVES

For this option, you'll want to put donation boxes in prominent places and post signage that says what items you're looking for and what they're going toward. The donated items are delivered to non-profits or charity organizations that distribute the items to people who need them. Donation drives can be simple to organize and extremely effective in getting stuff directly into the hands of those who need it most.

If you're organizing a donation drive for a nonprofit or charity, always, always, *always* check with someone first to be sure they need the items you're collecting. Some orgs are overwhelmed with donations and only have room for specific items. It can be wasteful if they need to sink extra time into organizing all the cans/shampoo/coats that people give but they don't need.

If you know for sure that your chosen nonprofit does need stuff, here are some ideas for donation drives:

- New and gently used coats to be donated to folks at a local homeless shelter
- Canned food for your local food bank

- Baby clothes and items for teen parent programs

- Pads and tampons for menstruating people in crisis situations (homeless services, disaster relief, refugee camps, women's jails)

- Personal care items for survivors of sexual assault in a hospital ER

- Holiday gifts for kids and families living in poverty

- Back-to-school supplies like pens and notebooks and backpacks for kids in need

- Old towels and blankets for animal shelters

A donation drive can be part of a larger campaign to raise awareness. Ten-year-old Amariyanna "Mari" Copeny (also known as Little Miss Flint) built on her work to bring attention to the water crisis in Flint, Michigan, by collaborating with Pack Your Back to raise over $10,000 worth of donations of backpacks and school supplies for her city's students.

DONATIONS OF SERVICES AND GOODS

Another way to use in-kind donations is to ask for good and services for your campaign or cause. This is also a great way to make connections with local businesses. You can approach owners by calling them, writing a letter, or just stopping in. I find that going to businesses with pre-printed letters requesting donations (because some business owners require a letter) and describing your campaign is really effective—it's hard to ignore a girl who walks into a business and asks for a donation in person! It shows you care and you're serious. Here are some examples of in-kind donations that you might get:

- Food from a restaurant or store for your events and meetings
- Professional photography or videography services
- Web design or graphic design
- Free advertising on radio or TV—public stations often donate slots for causes or nonprofits
- Craft supplies or printing of signs, flyers, or banners
- Office supplies or craft supplies
- Space to hold meetings or events (coffee houses, rec centers, places of worship)
- Swag (free stuff you can give out, like samples, pens, etc.)

Grants and Major Moolah

Grants are gifts of money that you never have to pay back—a.k.a. FREE CASH! Unlike individual donations given spontaneously, grants are typically scheduled to be given out on a regular basis (yearly, quarterly, etc.), and only to organizations or causes that "win" an application process. (You knew there'd be a catch, right?) But the juice is worth the squeeze: grant awards can range from as little as $500 to as much at $500,000 or more!

So how do you get a grant? You apply. The required application materials vary, but usually include statements of purpose, budget declarations, and a detailed plan of how you'll use the money. Think of it like a combination of a well-written crowdfunding campaign and a kickass college essay. There is definitely an art to writing grant applications, and many books and online sources give advice on doing so (check out grantland.org for tips and examples).

THE KEY TO WINNING GRANTS IS TELLING YOUR STORY, AND WHY YOUR CAUSE IS IMPORTANT, IN A TRUTHFUL AND COMPELLING WAY.

Remember to tell your story using persuasive words and imagery. (See Chapter 4 for a refresher.) That story helps you develop a relationship with grantmakers and funders—and ultimately get you that free money!

FINDING AND WRITING GRANTS

Applying for grants is one more way to fund your work. It's definitely not required and is seriously time consuming. But if you do it, all your work on your campaign plan and messaging will serve you well when making your case for funding.

Most grants are funded by individuals and groups interested in a particular social change, so they're usually for specific types of activism work. It can be challenging to find grants for feminist topics and community organizing. So let's start with how to even find grants in first place.

Start Local Open an internet search and type "grants" + "place you live" and see what comes up. Figure out who the funders are in your area and what kind of work they've funded in the past.

Search National Databases The Foundation Center is the most popular and widely used national database of available grants. Access is by paid subscription, but many public libraries provide free access to its online grant directory. Ask your local librarian.

Look for Social Justice Grants Grantmaking orgs that are specifically looking to fund feminist activist work are not as plentiful as grants for, say, scientific research or direct outreach services—but in some ways that makes them easier to look out for. These focused grantmakers also tend to be smaller than traditional foundations, and more rooted in grassroots thinking. The grants tend to be smaller—several thousand instead of hundreds of thousands of dollars—but definitely worth your time. Look up feminist foundations like the Third Wave Fund or social justice grants like Resist grants. Google "feminist grants" or "social justice grants."

Get Intense about Research Once you identify a few grants you may be eligible for, go deep. If the grant is offered by a nonprofit, you can look up all its financial details and lots of other info on Guidestar (guidestar.org). Look at its website and social media accounts, and take note of staff and news links about them. Then dive even deeper: What kinds of causes have they given money to? Knowing that will help you determine if they're a good fit for you and give you a head start on developing a relationship with them.

Partner with a Nonprofit Sometimes a grant application requires you to have nonprofit status to apply. If you don't want to build a formal nonprofit organization from the scratch (though you could; see page 149), partner with an existing nonprofit and apply with them as your "fiduciary agent." This means that the nonprofit will technically be the named recipient of the grant and will funnel the money through its organization to your campaign. The nonprofit assumes financial responsibility for your grant and your work, so it tends to take its "fiduciary agent" relationship pretty seriously, and so should you. But this option can really be worth it—it may open new grant opportunities or allow you to meet established activists who might mentor you. Go back to your "allies" list from your campaign plan brainstorming (page 58) and see if any might be a good fit.

Follow the Rules I don't often advise people to follow the rules to a T, but in this case, *follow the rules to a T.* If the grantmaker wants you to send a letter first (called a query letter), do it. If they want a specific form filed online or mailed, do it. They get a ton of applications, and the process is highly competitive. Skirt the rules and your application will go straight in the "discard" pile.

Take the "Report Back" Seriously When you receive a grant, you will usually be required to report back on how the funds were used and/or what you accomplished. It may seem like a lot to keep track of, but remember, *this is in exchange for free money.* You literally owe it to the grantmaker to report on your progress if requested. And if you're super successful, you may be able to have the grant extended or get funded for an additional year.

☆ ☆ ☆ ☆ # Takeaways ☆ ☆ ☆ ☆

1 Keep an eye on cash flow and income.

If you're unsure about your budgeting skills, try to learn a bit more about bookkeeping before you start fundraising. Could a parent or guardian explain how they make a budget? Do you know an accountant who could show you the ropes? Ask for a quick overview of the basics.

2 Get creative when it comes to donations.

Remember that donations don't have to be money. Which businesses, faith communities, and foundations in your area might be willing to contribute to your cause? Make a list that includes the item or resource you would like from each. Then work with an adult mentor to craft a strategy for approaching the owners or leaders and asking for their help.

3 Have fun fundraising!

Though raising money is serious, be sure to enjoy the process. Set up a strong team to support your efforts and ask for help when you need it. Every new thing you learn how to do gets you one step closer to being the change you want to see in the world (it's cliché but it's true!).

☆ ☆ ☆ ☆ ☆ ☆ ☆ ☆ ☆ ☆ ☆ ☆

Group Dynamics

AND Rallying Your Troops

To say that we need to come together in frightening political times is like saying: "The sky is blue." "The sun is hot." "Climate change will end the world." It's all so obvious. Working together is essential to organizing campaigns and to engaging in activism. We can do it alone, but we shouldn't have to and it doesn't make sense to. Let's get into how to organize groups, how to enlist people to volunteer for your cause, and how to partner with adults who support your work.

LET'S GET ORGANIZED! ❯

"We're all under the same sky and walk the same earth; we're alive together during the same moment."

MAXINE HONG KINGSTON, Chinese American author

In activism as in life, working with other people is essential. The quote on the previous page, which is from Maxine Hong Kingston's 1976 debut memoir, *The Woman Warrior: Memoir of a Girlhood among Ghosts,* is spoken by one female character to another in a moment of personal crisis. I think these words are also a reflection on universalism—the idea that we're all in this world together, even if this world is kind of a mess.

Right now your team might be a team of one: You. Maybe you're feeling overwhelmed by the idea of how to bring other people into your activism. But probably even more daunting is the thought of doing all this work by yourself. That's why you need to reach out for support.

Back in Chapter 2, we talked about squad goals, finding and working with a group of people on your campaign plan. Now let's dive a little deeper into why groups add power to your work, what to do to find and convince people to join you, and ways to keep your group meaningful for everyone involved.

From One to Many: The Co-Leadership Model

Back in college, I was part of a feminist campus group that was led by a co-leadership team—we had two or three co-directors at any given time. This model was meant to distribute power among several people, allowing more participants to have a say in how the group was organized and run. It also built a more equitable decision-making structure: No one of us could make big decisions without consulting the others.

It doesn't come without pitfalls, however. Sometimes one of your co-leaders may end up doing more work than the others; in that case, you'll need to talk it through and find solutions for sharing tasks equally. Despite some disadvantages, this model can work amazingly well—many hands can accomplish more work faster than any one person can do alone.

SHARED LEADERSHIP CAN BE A CHALLENGING YET REWARDING MODEL.

Two other leadership models are **hierarchical** (one leader, with others in roles such as vice president or associate director) and **decentralized** (no leaders at all). Whatever model you choose, getting a group together to tackle your issue is a tried-and-true strategy to Get. Stuff. Done. More people means you don't have to make all the decisions alone. Getting input and talking out ideas with trusted colleagues is extremely helpful.

You'll also benefit from the powerful social dynamic inherent in groups. You'll be with likeminded people who really "get" your activist work and want to help carry the load.

HOW MUCH HELP DO I NEED?

Now that you're sold on forming a leadership group, let's back up a little. Before you start dragging people off the street or go full recruiter mode on social media, you'll need to figure out what kind (and how many) co-leaders will best serve your cause. So ask:

What kind of leadership model do I want?

Will I be the sole leader? Or should I share leadership with another person or a team?

Will there be different levels of leadership?

Sometimes a group forms naturally, which is awesome. Maybe yours coalesced after a protest, or you go to school together, or you connected over a brilliant campaign on Facebook. Poof! Instant group! From there, you and your group members can figure out what role you each want to fill within the leadership team.

But when you're building a more intentional group from scratch, it's helpful to have a vision for your leadership group *before* you start recruiting. You'll be better able to attract members because people are more likely to join a group that has a clear objective and roles to fill. When considering co-leaders, think about:

- How big you want your leadership group to be

- What different leadership roles need to be filled

- What work you imagine the group doing

- What skills or expertise would be helpful in that work

- What tasks you need help with

- How you can help ensure that your group is racially and LGBT inclusive or reflects other marginalized identities

Asking for help

For leadership roles, you should approach people one-on-one based on their known strengths and interests. Reach out to friends, teachers, club members, classmates—everyone is flattered when asked to do something they're good at because it's an affirmation of their abilities. And giving them a fancy title like "Fundraising Chair" doesn't hurt either!

If no one jumps to mind, that's totally OK. Be on the lookout for any person who is really passionate and invested in helping you organize. Keep your leadership team in the back of your mind as you talk to and meet people who want to join your cause.

Leaders vs. Volunteers

A big question to ask before your recruiting gets too far along is, Do you need a *leadership* group, or do you really need *volunteers*?

If you've already planned a campaign and just need some hands on deck to complete tasks (make signs, show up at a one-time event, staff a phone bank), you probably need volunteers. But if you're coordinating multiple campaigns, managing of a lot of details and people, or planning any tactic that will take lots of work and time, you'll probably want co-leaders. Because you and your brain can't be everywhere at once.

There's no magic answer here, and it might take trial and error to find the right balance. Start with a small leadership team and appoint new roles as your campaigns and tactics grow and change.

HOW DO I FIND PEOPLE TO JOIN MY GROUP?

The first step in recruiting is to hold a *general-interest meeting*—a no-pressure way for people to drop by and learn about your cause. First, get the word out: hang posters at your school, post on social media, distribute flyers around your neighborhood. Invite the kid who sits next to you in homeroom. Invite your teammates. Cast a really wide net!

The goal of a general-interest meeting is to get people to join your group and attend your next planning meeting. The best way to ensure that interested people come back is to collect their info at the event via a sign-in sheet and to announce the next meeting date right then and there. Remember: the more specific your ask and the easier you make it to join your cause, the more likely people will take you up on your request.

If you haven't yet assigned leadership roles but are looking for top-level help, use this meeting to identify people with the skill sets you need and the willingness to take on bigger roles. Speak to them individually and gauge if they'd be up for it. You never know till you ask! See the checklist on the opposite page for tips on setting up your first big meeting.

WHAT IF TOO MANY PEOPLE WANT TO HELP?

What an excellent problem to have! But it's still a problem. It's not easy to plug hundreds of people into your work in a meaningful way. Plus sometimes volunteers are only *excited* about your work—they don't necessarily want to *do* anything, especially not the less sexy stuff like building a campaign plan or organizing logistics for a protest or sitting through planning meetings.

If a lot of people want to help but don't really want to be part of your core organizing efforts—what you have isn't a group of co-leaders, it's a *volunteer base*. Which is awesome! With some care

CHECKLIST FOR A
GENERAL-INTEREST MEETING

- [x] Accessible location (for transit and driving, as well as for people with disabilities or limited mobility)
- [x] Flyer/Invite with:
  - [x] Info about the cause with awareness, persuasion, and mobilization messaging (keep it brief)
  - [x] Date, time, location
  - [x] Contact person (you, probably)
  - [x] Contact info (yours, or create an email account specifically for your cause)
- [x] Snacks (and advertise this on your flyers and posts—people lurve free food!)
- [x] Nametags and markers (inexpensive sticker ones are perfect)
- [x] Agenda (printed for meeting or shown on a whiteboard or screen)
- [x] Literature/Info (about your cause—e.g., pamphlets, articles, video)
- [x] Sign In & Sign Up sheets (collect email and phone number for everyone so you can follow up after the meeting)
- [x] Next meeting date (announce the date and encourage people to come back)

and feeding (literally), and ideally with the support of your co-leaders, you can direct that volunteer base when it's time to mobilize.

But . . . there's a big but: Don't fall into the trap of letting every volunteer be a decision-maker, or thinking that you have to find a role for each one. It's better to be honest about what you really need and recruit for those roles. Volunteers feel frustrated when their work isn't valued, and they'll soon realize if you don't have stuff for them to do.

Remember, too, that volunteers may eventually become leaders. A few dedicated people will emerge, so keep an eye out for them. They're the ones who always speak up and offer to help with the crappy jobs. They share ideas and seem genuinely excited about doing even the small stuff.

Last thing: People have a tendency to gravitate toward passionate get-it-done types. So if you're finding that your core team is a little too similar to you and doesn't reflect the diversity of the larger group, step back to see if you're overlooking important folks without realizing it.

What If Nobody Shows Up?

It's totally OK—don't be discouraged! If only a few people came, that's great! In a small group, you can have a much more substantive meeting and spend time getting to know who showed up and why. You really only need a handful of people to do the hard work of organizing and decision-making. I'd rather have two totally invested and ready-to-go recruits than twenty lukewarm maybes any day.

If you're unable to find people to join your group, that doesn't mean your work won't be successful. A group is great, but there are other ways to work in partnership and get support. For example, you can ask a larger group to co-sponsor your action, or tie it in to a bigger event that's already happening in your community.

Creating Safer Spaces

Making activism **intersectional** is vital to our collective liberation (for more on intersectionality, see page 202). You can't help people without acknowledging the identities and struggles that each person faces. In group organizing, that means being careful to create meeting spaces where anyone can show up and, speak their mind without feeling judged or threatened.

SIMPLE IDEAS FOR SAFER SPACES

The reality is that no space is ever 100 percent safe for everyone, but we can make spaces *safer* through thoughtful organizing and facilitating. Here is a starting point.

Choose Accessible Meeting Spaces

This may sound like a lot for one place to fulfill, but many schools, houses of worship, lodges, restaurants, coffee shops, and recreation centers easily meet all these requirements.

- Make sure the physical space is accessible and comfortable to people who use wheelchairs or have difficulty standing for long periods.

- Have seating that can comfortably accommodate people of varying sizes (ideally chairs without armrests).

- Think about the proximity of parking to the meeting space if most people will drive there.

- Select a meeting place on a bus or subway route, or offer rides/carpools and note that on your flyers and posters.

- If you're inviting people whose native language isn't English, provide translators (which usually costs money, so take that into account when budgeting).

Brainstorm Ground Rules

Start the meeting with a brainstorm of shared ground rules for respectful conduct. This will set a welcoming tone and reinforce your shared values as you pursue your mission. See the opposite page for classic tried-and-true rules. Bonus: These are also good safe-space rules that are useful in situations both in and out of activism.

Give the Option to Share Preferred Pronouns

This is a way to make trans, gender nonbinary, and gender-noncomforming people feel welcome. Before introducing myself, I explain briefly what pronouns are and give examples (she/her, he/his, they/them), and then share mine. I make it clear that people can choose to share or not. Some people may not feel comfortable doing so, especially when they're unsure if it's safe to be out. Another way to make this step *not* feel mandatory is to have stickers with pronouns at the check-in table, or leave a place on nametags for people to write them in if they choose.

Use a Progressive Stack

A *stack* is a list that keeps track of who is next to speak at a meeting. A *progressive stack* prioritizes voices that are less likely to be heard. For example, if several people raise their hands to speak, the facilitator will call on the person who hasn't spoken. Or if there are a ton of people with their hands up, the facilitator will first call on those of marginalized identities. Be sure to explain that you're using a progressive stack, and what it is, so that participants understand how the speaking order is decided.

Classic Ground Rules

One Mic → Only one person will speak at a time, and people will not interrupt or have side conversations while a person is speaking.

Step Up, Step Back → People will note how much time and space they're taking up and push themselves to speak up more or participate less.

Be Aware of Your Bias → Don't assume stereotypes about people based on what they look, speak, or act like.

Speak for Yourself → Use "I" statements and avoid sweeping generalizations about another person/group or identity of people.

Assume Best Intentions → If someone says something or asks something without using the perfect term or phrasing, assume the person has good intentions.

Be Open to Being Checked → If someone says something and it comes out as offensive or inappropriate, they will be open to being gently corrected or redirected.

Oops!/Ouch! → When someone says something that hurts you, you can say "Ouch!" to indicate that it was hurtful. The person who said the thing that hurt you can then choose to respond "Oops!" to indicate they are sorry. At the least, the harmful comment doesn't go unchecked, and at the most, participants are opened up to dialogue about why something was hurtful.

The "Vegas" Rule → What happens in the meeting stays in the meeting. Private information or stories are considered confidential and are not to be shared outside of the group. Never "out" someone as LGBTQ or having a marginalized identity to others outside of the group.

Group Management 101:
Running an Effective Meeting

Have you ever been in a bad meeting? It's like a class that feels like it'll never end. So how do you run a meeting that's successful, in which people feel invested and are enthusiastic instead of bored and unengaged? In short, a good meeting is well planned and efficient—it's short (about an hour long), effective (a clear purpose and agenda), and leads to actionable outcomes (a clear goal).

This section presents planning tips that will help you make the most of your meetings, whether you're starting your new activist group, gathering community members to talk about an issue, or strategizing on a big campaign with community partners.

MAKE MEETINGS FUN!

Want people to *want* to come to your meetings? Fun it up and make them a good use of everyone's time.

Feed Their Minds and Their Mouths Free food is a draw—seriously! Food also automatically makes people more comfortable and sets a welcoming tone. Something about breaking bread together puts us more at ease. Food is a budget item (see page 143), but you can keep it cheap by making your meetings potlucks (i.e., everyone brings a dish). These are doubly good because people feel like they're contributing to the cause.

Be Super Duper Clear Don't be vague about what the meeting is about, what will be discussed, and why it's important to come. Put it right in your invite/flyer/email. But don't overdo it. No need to write an essay, just don't forget to provide context to entice people to come.

KICKASS ICEBREAKERS

Here are a few lead-off questions that I keep in my organizing toolbox because they work well with lots of different groups.

TO SET THE TONE

These focus the meeting on what you're about to do:

★ Why did you decide to come to this meeting? (Ideal for general interest meetings or community events and presentations)

★ What do you hope to get out of this meeting?

★ Where do you hope to see [the issue you're working on] in ten years?

FUN AND PERSONAL

These create a social atmosphere and are sure to inspire laughter:

★ When you were a little kid, what did you want to be when you grew up?

★ What's your favorite childhood TV show or movie?

★ If you could order food from any restaurant, what would you order and why?

★ If you won a free vacation to the destination of your choice, where would you go and why?

Make It Social and Chill If appropriate, schedule social time at the beginning of the meeting. Play background music. Arrange conversational seating. This is a great way for people to settle in and get to know one another. Just limit the length, and let people know ahead of time in case they'd rather skip the chit-chat.

Use Icebreakers These activities help people loosen up and get into meeting mode. They can be anything from a serious or silly question (see previous page for examples) to a game or improv exercise.

MEETING ROLES

A successful meeting will have a leadership team of assigned roles. You can assign them before the meeting or at the beginning of each meeting. At a minimum, you'll want to have someone serve as:

Facilitator This person is the meeting boss. They "run" the meeting, direct the agenda, lead group activities and discussions, ensure everyone is able to participate, encourage discussion, and open and close the meeting. This role can change with each meeting or be filled by the same person every time.

Note Taker This person is the scribe. They take notes (called minutes) and send them out after the meeting. This person may also be the one to send around a sign-in sheet to collect contact info for follow-up.

If possible, you might also assign these roles to members of your core group:

Timekeeper No, this person is not a time traveler. Their only superpower is to help the facilitator keep the meeting on track by keeping an eye on the clock. If the allotted time is running out for an agenda item, the timekeeper lets the facilitator know so that they can wrap it up and move on to the next topic.

Recorder This is an optional role that you can recruit in the moment if necessary. Unlike the note taker, this person keeps a visual representation of the meeting in real time during a group activity. For example, if you're doing a group power map brainstorm, this person could draw it on a whiteboard as you're discussing it. This frees up the facilitator to focus on leading during a group process activity.

Awesome Agendas

A well-planned agenda will keep your meeting from turning into a *Titanic*-length snoozefest. An agenda is a list of stuff to talk about during the meeting and needs a decision made by the group.

If you're organizing the meeting, create the agenda and send it out in advance. You can solicit items from group members or create a "consent agenda," in which you make the agenda at the meeting with everyone's input and agreement. Whichever method you choose, make sure your agenda has the following:

- the name of whoever needs to speak for each agenda item,

- a realistic amount of time (5 to 10 minutes is usually adequate) to discuss each item,

- and a total amount of time for the meeting once all the agenda items are added up.

Aim for an hour-long meeting. Any longer and it's hard to keep people's attention without having breaks and snacks. Also keep track of *action items*—things to do after the meeting. The note taker should record these items, and so should the person responsible for actually doing them. Always leave five minutes at the end of the meeting to review action items and pick the next meeting date. This keeps the group focused and moving forward.

MAKING GROUP DECISIONS

Even when people are being respectful and following the rules, they might have vastly different ideas about how to approach a problem. If the disagreement is about a judgment call that needs to be made fairly quickly, you may have to decide as a group rather than debate each opinion. Therefore, it's best to establish a method for making decisions as a unit beforehand.

Here are a few decision-making systems that work well for activist groups.

Consensus Everyone must agree on the course of action to move forward, and discussion continues until that consensus is reached. Although consensus is ideal, it's not always possible, so there are modified versions of this model. One is U-1 (unanimous minus one), meaning the consensus must be unanimous minus one possible dissenting group member.

Voting Many groups require a minimum number of members, called a *quorum*, in order to hold a vote. A quorum is usually about half the number of voting members. You can also set a minimum number of favorable votes needed to move forward with a decision—e.g., a two-thirds, or majority vote. For anything that will have major, lasting repercussions, you'll probably want at least two-thirds of the group on board. You can vote publicly, with a show of hands, or anonymously, by writing votes on paper and then tallying them up.

Participatory This system is useful when a decision affects some people in a group more than others. For example, if you're deciding whether to move to an office without gender-neutral restrooms, that decision would impact people who prefer a gender-neutral restroom more than those who have no opinion or stake in the matter. So when it comes time to decide, only those affected by the decision can participate in the decision-making process.

Handling Disagreement

It's kind of unavoidable that you won't all agree all the time, and that's OK. Disagreement is healthy! But navigating out of a disagreement can feel impossible, as if you're going to make people feel worse no matter what you do. That's why planning ahead matters so much. When a debate arises, go back to your ground rules (page 179). Remember to respect one another, use "I" statements, speak one at a time, maintain confidentiality, and use Oops!/Ouch! to address hurtful comments as they occur. Following these rules will help those involved feel like they're in control.

If things get overheated, take a break, get some air, water, and food, and then come back to the issue when you're all calmer. Sometimes long meetings just make people cranky! If the disagreement is really huge, schedule a separate meeting to devote fair time to discussing each side's points.

Nobody's free until everybody's free.

FANNIE LOU HAMER, African American civil rights activist

Supporting Volunteers

Volunteers give their time to your cause because they truly care, so they need to be respected and cultivated if you want to keep them around. Free labor is a gift—appreciate it!

One critical component of community organizing is building relationships, and that includes relationships with volunteers. You're likely a volunteer yourself if you're not being compensated for your activist work. Your co-leaders and core team are volunteers too. You may also have additional volunteers who are on your email list or show up at rallies and events or do specific tasks for your cause. Those are the volunteers you need to manage, direct, and support. They may not be the same people from campaign to campaign, event to event, or fundraiser to fundraiser, but you still need their help and they need yours too.

Here are some basic tips for managing your engaged, committed volunteers.

Be Honest and Clear The easiest way to lose a volunteer is to be unclear about the job you want them to do. ("Just, you know, help out and stuff" isn't the most inspiring call to action.) It's important to lay out the details about the volunteer work up front, especially if the job requires special skills or background or is time- or labor-intensive. Ask yourself:

What, specifically, will your volunteers be doing?

How long is the commitment (an hour/day/week/year)?

Who will volunteers report to (if not you)?

Will volunteers be working alone or with others?

Make Every Job Matter Even if the task seems small, like making phone calls or entering data into a spreadsheet, tell them how their time and efforts are specifically helping to meet your goals. When asking for help, don't frame it as "Help us enter data!"—that sounds like homework. Say something like, "Help us end LGBT discrimination!" Because that's ultimately what you're doing (and data entry is part of it). Be truthful about what the work is, but frame it in the context of the bigger goal to keep your volunteers motivated.

> ## ALL VOLUNTEERS WANT TO FEEL LIKE THEY'RE PART OF SOMETHING BIGGER THAN THEMSELVES, AND THEY WANT TO BE WITH OTHER LIKEMINDED PEOPLE.

Give Incentives for Showing Up You don't need a ton of money for swag to incentivize volunteers to work hard. If you have a bunch of money, great! Get T-shirts and buttons and whatever! But there are free and cheapish ways to bait the hook: Give public recognition to your volunteers on your social media, offer to write them a letter of recommendation for college or a job, or even sign off on their work as community service for a school requirement (this usually requires an adult). And, again, free food. It really does help!

Create Community Care Moments All volunteers want to feel like they're part of something bigger than themselves, and they want to be with other likeminded people. Whether you're doing a one-day phone bank or a long-term volunteer assignment, take the time to introduce your volunteers to one another. Set a coffee break or a snack time so they can mingle. Break the ice in fun ways when they arrive for instruction (see page 181). If your volunteers typically work alone

> **VOLUNTEERS GIVE THEIR TIME BECAUSE THEY CARE ABOUT YOUR CAUSE, SO MAKE SURE THEY KNOW WHAT A HUGE DIFFERENCE THEY'RE MAKING IN IT.**

or from home, invite them to a semiregular in-person get-to-gether to socialize. Set up a Facebook group or a Slack/WhatsApp/Discord group so your volunteers can meet and communicate online. Building a sense of community creates warm fuzzy happy feelings and makes your volunteers feel supported and connected!

Say Thank You More than anything else, volunteers need to feel like they are wanted and appreciated and doing helpful, import-ant work. Spend time with them while they're volunteering and thank them over and over and over again (you can never say thank you enough). Update them regularly about your campaign. Send a thank-you after they complete a volunteer shift—by email if you have a lot of volunteers, or a handwritten note if you want to make them feel really appreciated (and use some cute cards). Creating a culture of respect makes a volunteer much more motivated to come back again and again!

{ Talking to Your Parents or Guardians }

Everyone has a different relationship with their parents or guardians. Maybe you're super close; maybe you haven't talked in years. Maybe you live together; maybe you live separately. Maybe you see eye-to-eye on activism; maybe you're polar opposites on politics.

Family relationships are extremely complicated, and yours is unique to you. This section will probably be most useful if you have a supportive relationship with your parents or guardians. But even if you don't, there are takeaways you can use to get the adult support you need to proceed and succeed.

GETTING PARENTS TO LET YOU DO STUFF

When I first got into activism, my parents were a bit amused—like, what is all this feminism stuff and where did it come from? But I'm lucky—they've always been supportive and proud of me doing this type of work, even when they weren't so sure they totally understood it. That said, my parents and I haven't always seen eye-to-eye on everything, and we've had some major conflicts too.

If you're close to your parents, talk to them about all this stuff you're doing! They'll definitely notice that you're up to something, so don't leave them in the dark. Ideally, your parents will be proud of what you're doing and will want to support you 100 percent. Being honest and open is a big first step in securing that support.

So how to get your parents or guardians to buy into the girl resistance if they're not quite there yet? Remember that persuasion and awareness messaging we figured out in Chapter 5? Well, that knowledge will work in this case too! So get out your message triangle! Think about what you want to say before you even start the conversation.

Let's say you want to go to a march in a big city. You need your parents' or guardians' permission Here's how to get it:

1 **Earn their trust.** Prove that you won't hide things from them and that you want them to be informed about where you're going and who you'll be with. Don't lie. Stick to the facts.

2 **Show why it's important to you.** Use your awareness messaging and persuasion messaging to make it clear how serious this issue is and why you feel so strongly about taking action.

3 **Show them a detailed plan.** They'll probably have lots of questions. Show them your campaign plan (if applicable). Explain how you're getting to the rally, where you'll stay, what you'll do to protect your rights and safety, who the organizers are, and where you'll be going.

4 **Meet them where they are.** Talk to them maturely. Be calm. Don't accuse. Acknowledge that you know they worry about you and want you to be safe and that this may be difficult for them, but you can be trusted.

- **Recall the values they taught you** Your parents or guardians were your first moral compass. They taught you to stand up for what's right, to be strong and smart, to care about others. Remind them of the ideals, morals, and ethics they instilled in you.

- **Prepare for objections** Think ahead of reasoned, thoughtful responses to counter their fears.

- **Compromise if necessary** If you just can't get through, consider alternatives. What if they attend the rally with you? What if you called them every few hours? What if you left the demonstration early?

BUT WHAT IF THEY TOTALLY DISAGREE WITH YOU?

This question isn't easy to answer, and I have to be real here. This situation is pretty common, so don't feel like you're the only one it's ever happened to. Still, it's upsetting and frustrating and you need to know how to do what you feel you must to do in your heart without ruining your relationship with the people you probably need and rely on the most.

You can employ the previous strategies—preparing, persuading, showing them why it matters—and if you have a loving and trusting relationship, you may be able to reach a point where they support you and you all agree to disagree. You'll probably have to adjust your expectations and be happy with that.

There is a small chance you'll change their beliefs, but the reality is they probably just won't "get it" right away. Think about how

many years it took for them to absorb and learn the things they believe. They can't unlearn them in an instant or even in a year, but maybe they can take baby steps toward understanding and supporting you because they love you.

Your parents may even express being disappointed in or angry with you. I can't tell you what will happen in that case. So much depends on your relationship with them. It hurts because you love them and they're supposed to love you, unconditionally. I've come to understand that, in families where relationships are healthy and caring except for differences in beliefs, your parents are probably acting out of love. It doesn't feel like it, but it's true.

YOUR PARENTS MAY OUTRIGHT REJECT YOUR ACTIVIST WORK AND REFUSE TO SUPPORT YOU.

That doesn't mean you have to agree with them. It doesn't make it hurt any less. But being true to yourself will make your work worthwhile. Chances are, if you've made it this far into this book, you already know what kind of person you are and what you believe in. There's no way you can be someone else.

If you're not allowed to do your activism out in the world, you can do it privately, in your own way. You can join groups online. You can start groups online. You can take action from your phone or tablet. You can write, either for yourself or for sites on the internet. Find a supportive network in your real or virtual friends where you can be yourself and talk about the things that matter most to you.

Finding Other Adult Mentors

Maybe you don't have a parent or guardian in your life. This situation is quite common. According to the National Network for Youth, over 2 million youths every year, and approximately 46,000 youths on any given night, are without a home. If you're Black in an urban area or Native American in a rural area or an LGBTQ person anywhere, you're more likely to be experiencing homelessness in the United States.

There are also situations where young people don't have a good relationship with the parenting adults in their lives. They may leave an unhealthy family environment and become emancipated minors. If you can't find support within your family, don't feel like you have to go without a supportive adult in your life. See below for places to find help.

Places to Find a Mentor or Adult Ally

SCHOOL: Teachers, Coaches, Counselors, Mentors

OTHER TEEN ACTIVIST GROUPS: Peer and Adult Mentors, Organizing Partners

FEMINIST NONPROFITS AND GROUPS: Feminist Mentors, Organizing Partners

COLLEGE CLUBS AND DEPARTMENTS: Youth Activist Mentors, Organizing Partners

PLACES OF WORSHIP: Adult Mentors, Organizing Partners

When you approach a potential adult ally, keep these things in mind:

- You're asking for a favor, so make sure you know what it is.

  - Why do you want a mentor or adult ally?

  - Do you need help navigating 18-and-up stuff like election petitions or grant writing?

  - What are you hoping to get out of the relationship? Abstract guidance and wisdom or concrete stuff, like, say, rides to places?

  - What can you contribute? How can you thank them, give back, or make it worth their while to help?

- Respect their time. Like you, they're probably super busy, so be on top of communication, do the work you say you'll do, and make good use of the partnership.

- Take responsibility if you mess something up. You don't want them to do the work for you. You want their support in the work you're leading!

My mentor relationships have always been most effective when approached as a two-way street, like a partnership. I want to learn and be guided, but I also want to share and exchange cross-cultural and/or cross-generational information.

Traditionally, boys have more access to mentors who will open doors for them, propel their careers, and give them access and advice. Girls need to mentor and take care of one another, fostering mutually beneficial relationships that propel us all forward. So when a younger person comes looking for your advice and support, please help! That kind of supportive and radical mentorship is inherently feminist—and an activism unto itself.

☆ ☆ ☆ ☆ # Takeaways ☆ ☆ ☆ ☆

1 Help your volunteers get stuff done by being specific and supportive.

What do you want them to do? Make a list with tasks and assignments, and be sure to tell them how much of a time commitment you need. And don't forget to take care of them—snacks! T-shirts! Socializing and making friends!

2 Being a good leader means being organized, flexible, and empathetic.

How will you establish ground rules and enforce them—by yourself, by committee? Draft a list of rules and communicate them clearly to your volunteers. Developing an overall philosophy for upholding the dignity and safety of every one of your group members will ensure that all feel welcome, valued, and empowered to make change.

3 Share your activities with your parents, guardians, or adult mentors and earn their trust by connecting what you're doing to the values you share.

You take your activism seriously, and so should the people you look to for guidance and support. How can you show them that what you're doing is grounded in the way they taught you to respect and care for other people? If possible, engage in open, honest discussions so that everyone's views and concerns are heard and respected.

Speaking Up AND Standing With

Activism is about working toward justice and equality. As activists, we fight injustice and inequality with inclusion, equity, love, and power. Your work will bring you into contact with people who are not like you, whose identities are marginalized, pushed to the edges of society, not treated as important. Learning how to respect, listen to, and support those people—being an "ally"—is the heart of activism. It's using your power for justice, righting wrongs, and bringing down what stands in the way of love.

LET'S GET GOING! >

"What is needed is a realization that power without love is reckless and abusive, and that love without power is sentimental and anemic. Power at its best…is love implementing the demands of justice, and justice at its best is love correcting everything that stands against love."

REV. DR. MARTIN LUTHER KING JR., Black civil rights leader

Activists talk a lot about "love." Standing with love, fighting with love, being on the side of love. In activism, everything that is "against love" gets replaced, repaired, or removed—things like discrimination, hatred, poverty, racism. These are all rooted in treating people differently and unfairly because of who they are.

When undertaking any work for change, I often reflect on Dr. King's quote on the opposite page, from his 1967 speech "Where Do We Go from Here." Let's unpack what it means.

The first part means that power without caring and compassion is tyranny. It won't bring about justice or radical change. But for me, the second part is even more meaningful. Dr. King is urging us to do more than just love each other—we must back our words and feelings with strength and force.

We are all oppressed in some ways, and many of us have privilege in other ways. So before you dig deep into your activist work, dig deep within yourself to understand who you are and where you fit in to the systems of privilege and power that run the world.

This chapter will break down key terms and concepts, like *cultural identity*, *allyship*, and *intersectionality*, and show you how they are vital to feminist activism. Along the way you'll get lots of ideas, tips, and guidelines for navigating your own path to becoming the strongest ally you can be.

✳ ✳ ✳ Key Activism Terms ✳ ✳ ✳

Remember back in Chapter 1 when we were talking about *power dynamics*—how institutional power creates systems of inequity? We used the little baby and the man in the suit to explore how we live in a world with socially established and enforced ideas about who has power. We also learned how grassroots organizing pushes back against these ideas by harnessing individual power and transforming it into collective power.

Now let's give you the vocabulary you'll need to talk about society's problems and your activism in everyday life.

privilege a systemic advantage or right that a person has because they belong to a particular group or identity

oppression the state of systemic disadvantage that a person experiences because they belong to a particular group or identity

What they mean for you: As an activist, acknowledge areas where you are more privileged, and areas where you experience oppression. To help, review the privilege checklist on page 209.

equality the idea or state of all people being treated the same

equity the idea or state of everyone being treated fairly

What they mean for you: People use these two terms interchangeably, but they're not exactly the same. Vernon Wall, co-founder of the Social Justice Training Institute, explains the difference like this:

"Equality is providing everyone with a pair of shoes. Equity is providing everyone with a pair of shoes that fit." Sometimes equity means giving "more" to one group, but only so that they have what they need to overcome deep-rooted prejudices or historical disadvantages.

diversity the recognition and celebration of differences

inclusion the process of realizing and affirming that people are not all equal

What they mean for you: Diversity is about adding people to your activism who represent a wide range of backgrounds, viewpoints, and abilities. Inclusion is about looking hard at even your smallest decisions and then doing your best to make sure your activist movement is welcoming to join and accessible to all.

Words into Action

Let's say you need a meeting place for a planning committee. Your best friend offers her living room. But her house isn't on a public transportation line—making it hard for those without a car to get there. She also lives two flights up, with no elevator—making it almost impossible for someone who uses a wheelchair to attend. And she has limited seating—making it difficult for people of varying sizes to feel comfortable. You start to wonder, how many different people am I leaving out by picking this particular meeting place? Then you'll think of options and realize that meeting in your school auditorium or a library is more welcoming and accessible. That's inclusion!

intersectionality the theory that related systems of oppression and multiple identities constantly intersect (cross paths) to create an experience that draws on all those identities and oppressions at once

What it means for you: This is a complex subject so let's break it down, starting with how the term came about. The feminist theory of intersectionality was first presented by Black legal scholar Kimberlé Crenshaw back in 1989. In her paper, titled "Demarginalizing the Intersection of Race and Sex," Crenshaw built on Black feminist thought dating back to the 1800s, specifically the assertion by many Black women that their race could not be separated from their gender and that they suffered oppression because of both. They felt feminism that didn't take race into consideration failed Black women because it wasn't inclusive of the multiple ways they experience oppression.

In other words, inequality and injustice stem from the intersections of racism, sexism, classism, ableism, homophobia, transphobia, and other types of discrimination and hate. These threads are interwoven, and cannot be separated one from another, in systems of oppression. Activism that does not examine these varied aspects of a group's experience cannot be said to accurately represent that group.

When you're organizing for change, part of being a good activist and feminist is acknowledging your own structural privilege and considering how that might make your organizing oppressive or exclusionary to others. Acting intersectionally means acting with awareness of privilege in order to create equity.

Language is not neutral. It is not merely a vehicle which carries ideas. It is itself a shaper of ideas.

DALE SPENDER, Australian feminist scholar

Words into Action

Intersectionality can help you see how and why your campaign about one issue relates to many others. Take the Dakota Access Pipeline, which many Native Americans protested on the Standing Rock Sioux Reservation. That was an environmental issue—the pipeline could leak and damage the water supply. But it was also a spiritual and cultural issue—the developers were building on land the Native peoples held sacred. Ask yourself:

★ How does this cause affect my own intersecting identities?

★ How does it affect people whose identities I don't share?

★ Where are the voices of people directly affected by this work?

★ How do I make sure I'm listening to them?

BEYOND POLITICAL CORRECTNESS

Words are power. How we speak and refer to people can give them power or take it away. Our words indicate whether we respect and understand them. That's why it's important to educate yourself about the different identities that people call their own.

The reality is, we are not all equal. You must work to create spaces and practices that expose that reality and try to change it. Being inclusive isn't just about being polite or "politically correct." It's about respecting the fundamental qualities that make up another person. It's also about recognizing that marginalized identities are often oppressed and using our power to make space for those with less.

Knowing the different types of identities described on pages 204–207 will help you successfully navigate the world of activism.

⌃⌃ Marginalized Identities Mini-Glossary ⌃⌃

This list—by no means complete—is a good place to start. Keep in mind that any person may experience more than one identity, and many identities encompass even more specific categories within them. When you come across others you aren't familiar with, Google them.

Racial, Ethnic, and Cultural Identities

Black People who come from or descended from people from Africa; "Black" is often capitalized to show that Black identity is equal to other ethnic groups and not merely a descriptor of skin color. Because of being displaced by slavery in the U.S., many Black Americans do not know their family's specific country of origin (unlike white people, who are typically able to trace their roots to a European identity like Italian, German, or English); they may use the term "African American" to identify with an entire continent.

Hispanic People who descended from Spanish-speaking Latin American or Iberian regions (the part of Europe associated with Spain and Portugal). Hispanic people may or may not also identify as Latino/Latina/Latinx.

Latina/Latino People who descended from Latin America (Latina refers to women; Latino to men).

Latinx A gender-neutral term for people who descended from Latin America, pronounced "la-*teen*-ex" and originating from queer and trans communities; today it is used more commonly as a catchall.

Native American/American Indian/First Nation A member of the indigenous peoples of the Americas; a complex identity composed of many nations, tribes, states, and ethnic groups.

Asian People who descended from Asia (the world's largest and most populous continent). This term can describe people of Japanese, Indian, Thai, Sri Lankan, or Korean ethnicities.

Pacific Islander People who descended from the original peoples of Hawaii, Guam, Samoa, or other Pacific Islands.

People of Color An umbrella term for all people who are marginalized because of their race or ethnicity. Some criticize the term for focusing on skin color over cultural or individual identity. Abbreviated POC.

Ethnic & Cultural Acronyms

AMEMSA Stands for Arab, Middle Eastern, Muslim, and South Asian; used in organizing to bring together different ethnic, cultural, and religious communities with shared experiences of discrimination and oppression despite being racially and culturally diverse communities. (The acronym is sometimes criticized for not including Iranians, who don't fit into any of the AMEMSA identities.)

API Stands for Asian Pacific Islander; sometimes APA (Asian Pacific American) is used or some combination of those words, for various cultural and ethnic groups from the East Asian, Southeast Asian, Indian subcontinent or Pacific Islands, who sometimes organize together because of shared experiences of ethnic discrimination.

Sexual Orientation Identities

asexual A person who does not experience sexual and/or romantic attraction; a catchall term for a huge diversity of different asexual identities.

bisexual A person who is attracted to more than one gender; sometimes narrowly defined as being attracted to "men and women." Most bisexuals are open to dating people of many genders.

gay Sometimes a catchall term for all non-heterosexual identities, but mainly refers to men who are attracted to men.

lesbian A woman who is attracted to women.

pansexual A person who is attracted to people of all genders

queer Sometimes a catchall term for all non-heterosexual identities or used as a specific sexual orientation that means "not straight" and is defined by the person who claims the identity.

Gender Identities

agender A person who does not have a gender identity and doesn't identify as being on the gender spectrum at all; may or may not also identify as nonbinary and transgender

bigender A person who identifies as having two genders, which can be any two genders (not specifically male and female); may or may not identify as nonbinary and transgender.

cisgender A person whose gender identity corresponds to assigned sex at birth. (Being cisgender is not a marginalized identity—it's a privilege—but it is an important term to know regardless.)

nonbinary A person who doesn't identify as a binary gender (man or woman) and may or may not also identify as transgender; a catchall term for many different and more specific nonbinary identities.

transgender A person whose assigned sex at birth doesn't match their gender; sometimes used as a catchall term for all gender identities that are not cisgender.

Disability Identities

Neurodiverse/Neurodivergent A term used by people who have a non-normative neurological identity, including autism spectrum, dyslexia, attention deficit hyperactivity disorder, Tourette syndrome, and other non-neurotypical identities.

Identity-First A theory and language built around self-identifying as disabled as a source of pride because disability is central to a person's identity. (An example is saying "disabled people" or identifying as a "disabled person.")

People-First A theory and language built on self-identifying as a person with disabilities because a disability doesn't define a person's humanity. (An example is saying "people with disabilities" or "person using a wheelchair.") Many activists choose people-first language, unless someone with a disability prefers identity-first language.

Check Yourself Before You Wreck Yourself

Now that you know that privilege is a thing, what do you do about it? It's hard to deal with your own privilege if you don't even know you have it. You may not even realize that the things that feel totally "normal" to you and your way of life—like skin color, body type, or social class—can (and do) give you privilege.

First you'll need to determine *how* you have privilege. Then you'll be able to navigate activism with more sensitivity and emotional intelligence (which you really need for this kind of work). A good way to start is with a "privilege checklist," like the one on the opposite page. The first privilege checklist was created by women's studies teacher Dr. Peggy Macintosh in her paper "White Privilege: Unpacking the Invisible Knapsack," which was published in *Peace and Freedom* magazine in 1989. After reflecting on the ways that men use their male privilege without even being aware that they benefit from their gender, Macintosh came to the conclusion that she also benefited from unearned privilege just because she is white.

> **AS AN ACTIVIST, YOU'LL LIKELY REALIZE THAT YOU NEED TO GIVE UP SOME OF YOUR POWER WITHIN THE SYSTEM SO THAT OTHERS CAN BE HEARD.**

Since then, many activists have created privilege checklists on a range of topics, from non-disabled privilege to heterosexual privilege to thin privilege. These checklists (which are easily available on the internet) show ways that you benefit from privilege by pointing out how others are oppressed.

PRIVILEGE CHECKLIST

Privilege checklists help you identify points of connection with other people and realize that what you may consider normal life isn't normal for everyone. Consider the following situations: Which apply to you? Which don't? Where do or don't you have privilege?

- ✓ I don't have to miss school to celebrate my religious holidays.

- ✓ I can use a public bathroom without being stared at.

- ✓ I'm expected to go to college, and my parents are helping pay for part or all of it.

- ✓ I feel like the police are here to protect me.

- ✓ If I turn on Netflix, I know I can find multiple movies about someone who shares my identity and cultural background.

- ✓ I can go to any stores, restaurants, or theaters without having to see if there's an accessible entrance.

- ✓ I get an allowance from my parents.

- ✓ I can find clothes that fit my body in most mainstream stores.

- ✓ I've had regular checkups my whole life, and when I get sick, I can easily go to the doctor.

- ✓ I can wear clothing or jewelry from my faith tradition without being teased or threatened.

- ✓ In the summer, I take vacations, go to sleepaway camp, or just hang out instead of getting a job.

- ✓ I can take whoever I want to a school dance without getting teased, stared at, or threatened.

Having privilege isn't something to be ashamed of. It's something to be aware of, to consider every time you act so that you don't unintentionally hurt others.

You may also sometimes experience privilege and oppression in the same identity. I self-identify as fat, in a body-positive way. I definitely experience oppression because of the size of my body, but I also experience privilege. I can still fit in airplane seats and shop at the mall. People don't assume I'm unlovable because of my size. But for some fat people, those injustices are their reality.

When dealing with our own areas of privilege and oppression, it's normal to feel emotionally uncomfortable. That discomfort invites change and growth. Resisting the discomfort may lead you to ignore an opportunity to learn and connect with others, which is itself a symptom of privilege. Doing this difficult, deeply personal, and self-reflective work can make your activism all the more meaningful.

Mansplaining

Maybe you've heard this term before? If you haven't, it's just what it sounds like: men explaining things to women that we *already know*. This phenomenon stems directly from male privilege. This gender privilege often translates into men taking up the most space in a conversation. Men assume they're smarter and more articulate than women because our society reinforces that they are. As a result, men speak over women in meetings or tell us what we know in a condescending way or put all the focus on their experiences and opinions.

Being a Good Ally

Everything in this book has been leading up to one thing: how to be an ally. We explored what makes a person marginalized. Then we worked on understanding what makes a person marginalized differently from the way you're marginalized.

Good intentions aren't enough. You can support a cause without being an ally to it.

Allyship is only helpful to marginalized communities when those allies combine love with their power to bring about justice. Allies are critically important to activist movements because they use their privilege, and their power, to help people affected by issues that the allies are not directly affected by.

Allies can turn the tide by putting their voices alongside marginalized voices of the people who are directly affected. Allies can reach others who might not care about an issue that doesn't affect them directly. Allies can stand behind folks who have been doing the work for a long time and amplify their message.

FIVE WAYS TO DO ALLYSHIP

1 **Pass the Mic** When given a platform to speak on an issue that doesn't directly affect you, hand off the opportunity to someone who is directly affected. And never take the mic from a group or person who's directly affected.

2 **Practice Bystander Intervention** When you see someone being bullied or harassed, definitely say something, but never assume that person needs you to fight their battles. In fact, drawing attention could make them more uncomfortable, or your interaction could escalate and make the situation even more dangerous. A bet-

ter option is bystander intervention: Ignore the harasser, and speak directly to the person, asking if they're OK. Offer to walk or sit with them. If someone is being harassed by a stranger in a public place, pretend you know them and strike up a conversation. These tips also work when friends (or strangers) are being sexually harassed at a party or event and you want to get them out fast.

3 **Speak Up, Not Over** As an ally but also a person with privilege, never assume you know what someone else wants. Educate people about injustice, but don't speak out before you've spoken with and invited people who are directly affected to share their experience.

4 **Listen Deeply** When a person who is marginalized speaks about an issue that affects them, believe and listen to them. Your opinion as an ally is not as valid as the lived experience of the person affected by that oppression. You can disagree, but don't drag them into a debate. It's fine if there are lots of opposing ideas within an identity or community, but it's not your job to decide and explain who's right or wrong.

5 **Educate Yourself** Maybe you're interested in learning about the experiences of a person with identities different from yours. Don't ask that person to educate you—that takes a lot of their time and effort. Find the answers on your own! Research on the internet so that next time you'll know. Even better, you won't make the person uncomfortable by asking deeply personal questions.

I raise my voice not so that I can shout, but so that those without a voice can be heard.

MALALA YOUSAFZAI, Pakistani activist and Nobel Peace Prize winner

‹ ‹ ‹ ‹ ‹ ‹ ‹ Microaggressions › › › › › › › ›

Has someone ever said or done something that was a little bit of-fensive but not overtly cruel? Like, a boy assuming you can't carry something heavy? Or if you're a POC, a person commenting on your hair or body that felt kind of racist? Or overhearing someone saying some racist BS to someone else? The kind of stuff that makes you roll your eyes and go, "Ugh!"

These are all examples of *microaggressions*. They're the little, everyday interactions in which, whether on purpose or by accident, people act or speak or create situations that are hostile or deroga-tory toward those with marginalized identities. They may be small, but they add up, and they're what makes oppression exhausting. The term was coined in 1970 by Black scholar and Harvard Medi-cal School psychiatrist Dr. Chester Pierce. He wanted to give a name to the daily insults and discrimination he endured and saw non-Black people carry out toward Black people. Microaggressions are often about race, but the term now encompasses the many ways that people of all marginalized identities experience constant discrimi-nation in tiny but hurtful ways.

Many times, people don't mean to be offensive and genuinely don't realize what's they've said. But we can't ignore it. The only way to stop microaggressions is to call them out when you see or hear them.

Though it's important to stand up against injustice, always protect your personal safety. Some people don't take well to being called out. That sensitivity is known as fragility, and it comes from having so much privilege that even a little criticism becomes a huge deal.

Here are some tactics to use. They are most appropriate when talking to people you have a relationship with: friends, family, peers.

Tactic: Ask the person to explain themselves.

Say: "I don't get it. What do you mean?"

★ *Watch them fumble trying to explain why their transphobic or racist or sexist joke is funny. Keep at it until they either give up or admit it was offensive.*

Tactic: Appeal to their ego.

Say: "I'm sure you know that [THE SEXIST TERM] is considered hurtful and offensive, so you probably don't want to go around saying it."

★ *Make it hard for the person to get defensive by spinning it as them being in the know, just merely forgetting.*

Tactic: Rely on their good character.

Say: "You're a really caring person and I know you wouldn't want to hurt someone. Saying [ABLEIST THING] is really offensive."

★ *Remind the person that you respect them while you correct them.*

Tactic: Remind them of their values.

Say: "Remember how our grandparents always set a good example by being kind to everyone, even strangers?" or "You know how the Bible says to love each other unconditionally?"

★ *When the person shares common values with you, remind them what those values are.*

Tactic: Aim at the action, not the person.

Say: "That's a racist thing to say,"

★ *Avoid name-calling if you really want to get through to them. Saying "You're a racist" will only make them defensive.*

WHAT TO DO IF <u>YOU'RE</u> CALLED OUT

Everyone makes mistakes—the important thing is to learn from those mistakes and change for the better. Here are ways to handle yourself in a respectful and welcoming way.

1 **<u>Don't get defensive.</u>** Be willing to sit with the discomfort. Choosing defensiveness only makes the situation worse.

2 **<u>Really listen.</u>** Hear what they're saying with an open heart. Don't try to explain it away or speak over the person we've hurt.

3 **<u>Apologize.</u>** Don't hedge. Avoid equivocations like "I'm sorry if your feelings were hurt . . . " You hurt them, now own it.

4 **<u>Understand that it's about more than feelings.</u>** Don't minimize oppression by accusing someone of "being emotional." A comment or action that seems like nothing to you can be huge to someone else.

5 **<u>Don't bring in your own feelings.</u>** Take time to figure out why you made this mistake. Just don't make it all about your guilt, which centers you instead of the person you hurt.

6 **<u>Don't "tone police."</u>** Has an adult ever refused to discuss something until you "calm down" or "act like a grown-up"? Yeah, that sucks. Refusing to listen or engage with someone until you feel like they sound or act calm/rational/polite is known as tone policing. When it comes to social justice, nobody owes you politeness, and polite talk isn't the only way to discuss issues.

7 **<u>Avoid excuses.</u>** "But I have a gay friend!" Um, good for you? Having friends with marginalized identities doesn't give you license to say hurtful things.

8 **<u>Commit to doing better.</u>** Promise to change your behavior, and then follow through.

☆ ☆ ☆ ☆ *Takeaways* ☆ ☆ ☆ ☆

1 Everyone experiences different forms of privilege and oppression because of how they identify and present in the world.

Having privilege isn't something to be ashamed of—it's something to be *aware* of. Commit to considering your own privilege and/or the oppression of others before you act or speak. What can you do differently to positively affect another person or group? If you experience microaggressions, how can you let others know or understand your feelings? Talk with people who feel similarly to come up with strategies that can benefit everyone.

2 Words matter because they shape how we think.

Being an ally means respecting language. When talking to other people, use their preferred pronouns and identifiers to describe them. Work on ways to encourage your friends or family to be more sensitive when interacting with people who are different from them.

3 You might mess up. And that's okay.

See mistakes, as uncomfortable as they are, as a learning opportunity. Admit that you goofed up, apologize sincerely for the hurt you caused, and move on with the intention to do better. When you're alone, reflect on what happened, but don't beat yourself up. Be as kind and understanding with yourself as you try to be with others.

Caring FOR Yourself AND Your Community

Girls can only lead the resistance if we take care of ourselves and each other. Part of taking care of the world around you is taking care of yourself. "Self-care" is simply the act of giving your body and mind what they need, whether that's rest, recreation, food, or Netflix. It's a survival strategy that serves our activism goals because it allows us to thrive and keep on fighting. When life feels overwhelming, be sure to give yourself the break and the balance you need.

LET'S GET FUELED UP! >

"Caring for myself is not self-indulgence. It is self-preservation, and that is an act of political warfare."

AUDRE LORDE, American feminist activist and writer, in *A Burst of Light*

Activism can add myriad stresses and anxieties to your life. Making change is part of what makes us feel good, empowered, and in control of the unfairness in the world. But all the emotional and physical labor of activism can take a lot out of you. There are the meetings, phone calls, social media, learning, teaching, speaking, and on and on. There's the constant onslaught of terrible things happening every second of every day.

Add to that all your regular everyday stuff: school, family, friends, jobs. Layered on top of all of it are the daily oppressions that we face at the intersections of our identities: sexism, racism, classism, ableism, homophobia, transphobia, and other kinds of discrimination. And it's not all in your head, so don't let anyone tell you it is. Studies have shown that nearly everyone from a marginalized identity is feeling record-high levels of stress, and that over twice as many teenagers are reporting "feeling overwhelmed" compared to twenty years ago. So after helping others, how do we help ourselves?

This chapter is all about the important work of keeping yourself physically and mentally healthy. The results will be a happier, more balanced you!

Make a Self-Care Plan

Activism is hard work. You're no good to the girl resistance if you're burned out, cranky, and exhausted. Your cause matters. But so do you. Caring for the whole you—your body, mind, and heart—matters. A plan for self-care forces you to think about specific strategies and how to do them, not just wave them off with a "Yeah, I'll sleep eventually." (Hint: "eventually" will never come.)

Think in campaign-planning terms: start with the strategy, not the tactic. The goal is to get you feeling fresh and ready to get back into resistance mode. The target is you. Your strategies depend on what helps you relax and what resources you have. Your resources may be time, family, friends, media, money, or your cozy bed. Then figure out what to do by making a plan.

START WITH A MIND MAP

Remember the mind maps you used to choose an issue in Chapter 2? Now you'll that same tool to create a self-care plan.

Start by drawing four circles and label them TRIGGERS, MIND, BODY, and SUPPORT NETWORK.

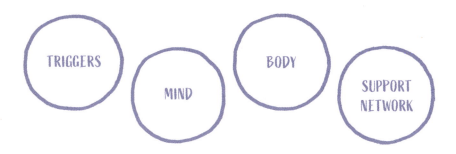

Triggers First we'll start with what makes you feel bad. What gets under your skin, makes you seethe with rage, feel scared or afraid? Write them around the TRIGGERS circle.

Now let's identify what makes you feel good! What are the activities that help you relax, chill out, or unwind? Separate these into the MIND and BODY circles.

Mind activities nourish your mental and emotional health: reading a book, watching a movie, playing a game on your phone, listening to music.

Body activities nourish your body: yoga, walking a dog, painting your nails, making a cup of fancy tea, or even straight-up sleeping.

Support network is made up of people to whom you can go for advice: teachers, friends, family members, coaches, clergy leaders, bosses, your cat. (Cats are people, too.) Remember that different people provide different support. Write these people around the SUPPORT NETWORK circle.

Now, look at your plan: Do you see a lack of support or activities that take care of your mental or physical health? What can you do in those areas? What people or communities can you connect with? Write down what you can do to improve those areas. Then put your self-care plan somewhere you can look at it regularly. If you don't accomplish these goals all the time, it's fine. Self-care shouldn't be an additional stressor—if it is, then don't do that particular strategy. Reach out to your support network. Schedule a friend date. Call a hotline.

Everyone struggles. You are not alone. And you certainly don't have to figure it out all by yourself.

THE POWER OF JOURNALING

Journaling is the process of recording your daily thoughts, feels, doodles, or whatever. It can help you process and reflect, and it creates a record of your progress over time. If you're holding on to a lot of anxiety and bad mood stuff, write it out. Don't edit yourself. Just note down all the positive things in your life, however small. Remember that we can hold the good and the bad in our hearts at the same time. Sometimes we just forget about the good.

Journaling doesn't have to be a physical diary or even handwritten. It can be typed in a Word doc or on Tumblr or a blog. It can be text or drawings or poems or collages or anything that helps you get thoughts out of your head. Here are some ideas to get you started.

Gold Star Checklist: You know how little kids get star stickers to track good behavior? Make a grown-up version. List all the stuff you did in a day, big and small, and do that every day (or every week). It'll help you focus on everything you *are* doing well instead of the things you still need to do. What did you do today that warrants a gold star?

Did you eat breakfast? Gold star!

Did you organize a rally? Gold star!

Did you finish your homework? Gold star!

Did you take down the patriarchy? Gold star!

Prompts: Ask yourself a self-care question and write about it:

- What is my favorite thing about myself?

- What does my ideal world look like and feel like?

- I am grateful for . . .

- My happiest moment this week was . . .

- I was inspired today by . . .

Create a Tracker: Make a section in your journal to track how often you accomplish your self-care goals. You'll be more likely to hold yourself accountable if you have to check something off, and will helps keep track of what's going on with your self-care habits.

Thank You, Me: Write a thank-you note to . . . yourself! Thank *you* for all the things you do for you, every day: for your own safety, health, wellbeing, and benefit. Nobody takes care of you like you do!

The Self-Care Selfie

Some people think selfies are vain and silly. Wrong! Selfies are a way for us girls to literally make our own picture of ourselves and put it into the world (if we choose to). So don't let anyone make you feel ashamed about them.

In fact, self-portraits are powerful tools for self-reflection, self-care, and resistance. For centuries, women have been using self-portraits to exert control over their bodies and narratives. Take Mexican painter and activist Frida Kahlo. In her many self-portraits she examined topics of bodily autonomy, gender, sickness, power, and colonialism. Selfies are just the modern version of self-portraits like Kahlo's.

Whether or not you share your selfies, they can be part of your self-care plan. In a world that's constantly telling girls we're unattractive and not good enough, sometimes snapping a selfie is the pick-me-up we need. So next time you're ready for a selfie, take a few seconds to reflect on all the things you love about yourself and all the good you do in the world. Then snap on!

CHEAP AND EASY SELF-CARE IDEAS

Try these low-cost and free ideas that you can do by yourself or with your friends.

Go Play: Channel your inner child. Color an adult coloring book (or a kid one), build a Lego kit, make glitter slime, do a puzzle, go swing! Got a small kid (or a pet) in your life? Play with them!

Get Streaming: Basic subscriptions to many popular streaming sites like Hulu and Netflix cost under $10, and many offer free trials. You can also find a lot of free (and legal) movies on YouTube.

Visit the Library: Take out a good book (see the Resistance Reading List on page 228). Libraries also lend out movies and magazines and music, plus some have cool digital archives to explore at will. Also, they're quiet and have comfy chairs for working distraction free. If you can't get to one, most offer e-books you can download and "borrow" for the usual lending period.

Create a Stress-Free Zone: Have a DIY relaxation experience. Light a candle or incense or use essential oils or your favorite cologne. Turn on relaxation music. Then do whatever feels good. Dancing, yoga, stretching, or just being perfectly still.

Get into Nature: Take a trip to a nearby park or just tour your own neighborhood. There's something about getting your body moving that helps your brain clear away negativity.

Scrub-a-Dub-Dub: A shower or bath can be the perfect thing when you need to literally strip down and just be with yourself. Also a great place to wiggle around to some music, or do a mini-meditation.

Unplug Totally: Most of us don't even realize how attached we are to our devices. If it doesn't cause you too much anxiety, try turning off your phone and all electronics for a day, an hour, or more. It'll be weird at first, but you'll probably feel more connected to yourself and what you actually want and need in your life.

Take a Nap: #sleeptight

Resistance Reading List

Reading has always been my favorite way to escape from reality and when I'm doing self-care best, I'm making time to read—for myself, not for work or for school or for a project. Here are some books for your leisure-time reading list, curated for you by me.

NONFICTION

Here We Are: Feminism for the Real World edited by Kelly Jensen

You Don't Have to Like Me: Essays on Growing Up, Speaking Out, and Finding Feminism by Alida Nugent

Bad Feminist by Roxane Gay

Being Jazz: My Life as a (Transgender) Teen by Jazz Jennings

Full Frontal Feminism: A Young Woman's Guide to Why Feminism Matters by Jessica Valenti

Redefining Realness: My Path to Womanhood, Identity, Love, and So Much More by Janet Mock

CLASSICS

Sister Outsider: Essays and Speeches by Audre Lorde

The Handmaid's Tale by Margaret Atwood

Feminism Is for Everybody: Passionate Politics by bell hooks

A Room of One's Own by Virginia Woolf

Women, Race, and Class by Angela Davis

The House on Mango Street by Sandra Cisneros

Community Care as Self-Care

So often, self-care advice is "Go to the spa! Get a manicure! Eat a brownie!" Sure, do those things if they work for you and you can afford them. But self-care goes deeper, and it's not always about spending money.

There are many reasons why self-care isn't as easy as splurging for a spa day. Not having enough money for basic needs is a huge stress and makes it hard to imagine doing something good for yourself. Discrimination can make you think you are unworthy of caring for yourself. Anxiety or depression may hinder you from coping with the world, sending you down a spiral of guilt and apathy.

Enter: *community care.* Community care is the idea that you can't do self-care on your own. You will need someone to hold you accountable and help you find the physical or mental space. Community care stems from the radical notion that isolating ourselves isn't always the best way to recharge—that sometimes together we can help each other feel better.

Have you ever had a really good conversation with someone? Like, really, really good. That's what community care can feel like.

FIVE IDEAS FOR COMMUNITY CARE

1 **Talk to people.** Community care can be as simple as calling up a friend and asking how they're doing or sending a message letting them know you're thinking about them. After the massacre at the Latinx gay nightclub in Pulse, Orlando, many straight allies reached out to me (and I assume other LGBTQI people) with messages of support. Likewise, I reached out to my Latinx friends with open messages of support.

2 **Host a party.** Arrange a get-together with other activists, like a night of board games or a sleepover or meeting up for dinner or coffee. I used to take part in a drop-in feminist coffee group once a week. Sometimes I'd be so tired that I didn't think I had the energy to go, but I always left feeling reenergized.

3 **Respect boundaries.** Community care is powerful and fun, but for some people socializing can cause more stress, not less. Introverts burn out too, so if you're not feeling the group scene, make sure to ask others to respect your personal boundaries. On the flip side, always respect other people's boundaries too. Don't pressure them to be in a community space or to do more work, even if it needs to get done.

4 **Schedule a date.** Ask someone you trust to check in on you and make sure self-care is happening regularly—and offer to do the same for them. For example, make a date with your closest friend to take a quiet walk or read in a park or binge-watch a favorite show.

5 **Turn activism into community care.** The most marginalized people and communities are also the ones who struggle with finding time and resources for self-care. Part of your activism could be organizing self-care activities for others. You can donate skills— offer to teach a free community class about something you know. Gather people with similar interests and experiences. Organize a feminist club around an activity, like a stitch-and-bitch knitting circle or a trans yoga class or a wheelchair basketball club or a queer writer's workshop. You can teach others about self-care and community care and why they're important. It may not seem as radical as holding a rally or packing a courthouse to demand justice, but it's just as important as any of those things.

It's Normal to Feel How You Feel

When you are really invested in a cause, that engagement may cause you to experience trauma: either because the problem affects you directly or because it affects someone you care about. This is called **secondary trauma** or **vicarious trauma**—when your work with other people who are experiencing trauma starts to rub off on your own emotional health.

You may also get fed up and tired from being fed up and tired all the time. This feeling is called **compassion fatigue**. If not dealt with, compassion fatigue can lead to burnout, and that's no good. We can't do activist work if we're too exhausted to care or think.

Before you know it, you're hurtling towards **activist burnout**, the feeling of being too stressed to function in a healthy way emotionally, physically, and/or spiritually. When stress and trauma become part of our everyday life, they can start to feel normal-ish, making it harder to identify what's keeping you down.

You might be on the edge of activist burnout if you feel

- Extremely tired
- Unable to sleep
- Anxious or jumpy
- Guilty or shameful
- Like you can't focus
- Like you can't do anything right
- Sad or depressed

- Angry at yourself and/or others
- Grumpy and impatient
- Lonely or alone
- Unable to see the good
- Physically ill or nauseous
- Soreness or constantly in pain

It's normal if you feel like you can't deal with these problems or feelings on your own. But it's important to notice how they are affecting you:

Are you experiencing them more intensely, or more often, than usual?

Do they seem too hard to deal with?

Most important: Do not ignore them. Fortunately, many free resources are available to you. There's never shame in dealing with your emotional and physical health—even if it takes time, even if it means you have to stop doing your activism for a while, even if it means asking for professional help. See "You Are Not Alone" below for where to go if you need to talk to someone right now.

You Are Not Alone

Many of these hotlines also have text and chat options online.

National Suicide Prevention Helpline: 1-800-273-8255

National Suicide Hotline: 1-800-SUICIDE

Teen Line (Teen-to-Teen Support): 1-800-TLC-TEEN

Trevor Project (LGBTQ Youth) Lifeline: 1-866-488-7386

Trans Lifeline: 1-877-565-8860

National Sexual Assault Hotline: 1-800-656-4673

National Domestic Violence Hotline: 1-800-799-7233

Remember: Someone is always there to listen. <3

☆ ☆ ☆ ☆ Takeaways ☆ ☆ ☆ ☆

1 Activism isn't easy.

You can't do your best if you're coming apart at the seams. If you're drained or distracted, it's time to recharge. What makes you feel relaxed or refreshed? Who can you talk to for advice or as a sounding board? Don't ignore the warning signs of burnout and fatigue.

2 You don't have to justify the way you feel.

Feelings don't have to be rational to be valid, and telling yourself you "should" or "shouldn't" feel a certain way will only make you miserable. If you're tired, you're tired. If you're mad, you're mad. If you're happy, you're happy. That's just how feelings work!

3 Give your body—and your brain!—a break.

Eat healthy (and tasty!) food, listen to music, journal, take selfies, or just zone out. Self-care is powerful and necessary. Always remember and never forget—you are worth taking care of.

Now get out there and resist!

☆ ☆ ☆ ☆ ☆ ☆ ☆ ☆ ☆ ☆ ☆

ACTIVIST GLOSSARY

Whether you're new to activism or already fighting, you might not be familiar with all the terms in this book. Here are definitions to power up your resistance.

activism Work that strives to change the balance of power in favor of more just treatment for all

agenda A list of things to talk about in a meeting

allies People working towards (or sympathetic to) the same cause as you

allyship The act of respecting, listening to, and supporting people whose marginalizations aren't the same as yours

ask The thing you're, well, asking people for, such as a donation, a vote on an issue, a signature on a petition, etc. (e.g., "make the ask")

bird-dogging Following an elected official at events and politely (but insistently) speaking up about your issue and/or asking questions

budget An estimate of and plan for managing your organization's income and expenses

call to action A prompt for a person to take a specific action (e.g., "call your legislator" or "join as a volunteer")

campaign plan The map for running an activist campaign, including goals, targets, tactics, resources

cash flow The amount of money going in or out of your organization. Negative cash flow means you're losing and/or owe money

co-leadership A group management system in which decisions and oversight are shared by two or more people

demonstrations Any tactic that takes place in public to get people's attention, such as a rally, march, or flash mob

district office The office your elected official keeps in their home district (i.e., the one in your state, city, or county, as opposed to the one in Washington DC)

fiduciary agent A nonprofit partner for your campaign that will receive a grant on your behalf (so you don't have to form your own nonprofit)

501(c)(3) A not-for-profit organization that is exempt from paying federal taxes

gender binary The idea that there are only two genders instead of the expanse of gender identities

gender norms The idea that a person's interests and abilities are dictated by their gender

grant A monetary gift administered to an organization from a foundation or individual donor, selected based on application materials

grassroots organizing Activism that harnesses the power of groups to pressure people in power to change policies and practices

hierarchical leadership A group management system in which one person heads everything, with others in supporting roles

implicit bias Assuming something about a person because of stereotypes about their race, gender, social class, ability, etc.

in-kind donation A nonmonetary contribution to your organization (goods, supplies, or services)

intersectionality The theory that a person's multiple identities can intersect and create a lived experience that draws on all those identities and the oppressions that affect them

institutional power Power that comes through or with a job, position, money, identity, or status

leave-behind Printed material with a summary of your cause and asks, along with contact info for your group

lobbying Visiting or writing to an elected official demanding (politely) that they take action on specific legislation

marginalization the oppression and social disadvantages experienced by people who are not in the dominant group

microaggression Small, everyday interactions that reinforce stereotypes or otherwise create a hostile environment for people with marginalized identities

mobilization The messaging stage that gets people to take action in support of your cause

net profit/net loss The amount of money that you have or that you owe after subtracting your expenses from your income

oppression Systemic disadvantages that a person experiences because they belong to a particular group or identity

patriarchy A power hierarchy in which men have the most structural privilege, and women and nonbinary people are below them

petitions Documents with a statement or demand signed by supportive people

phone bank Organized phone calls made to specific people to get their opinion, ask them to take action, or solicit donations

press release A brief document that describes a newsworthy development in your cause (such as an event announcement) to be sent to media outlets

privilege Systemic advantages that a person receives because they belong to a particular group or identity (e.g., male privilege, white privilege)

query letter An initial letter sent as part of a grant application before more materials are considered

rape culture The set of social and cultural ideas, images, and practices that normalize sexual violence against women

safer space An environment where people can speak their mind without feeling judged or threatened

secondary target Someone who can't make the change you want, but who has influence over people who do

social pressure Motivating people to take action by showing how their peers have already done so; e.g., "I Voted" stickers or social media "challenges"

tactics The actual action of your activism, such as petitions, marches, protests, donor drives, and the like

talking points Prepared facts, statements, or arguments to have handy anytime someone asks about your cause

target A person with the power to help your cause, or a person who stands in the way of your cause

topline messages The two or three most important mini-messages that you want people to hear and take away

INDEX

Acknowledgments

• • •

This book wouldn't exist without Waffle, my partner and co-adventurer and chief executive of parenting. Thank you for the days and nights you sacrificed so I could write and for every time you kept me fed, caffeinated, and motivated. I still don't know how this book got done, but I know it's at least 90% because of having a Waffle in my life. Thanks to my entire publishing team at Quirk Books, particularly my editor Blair Thornburgh, whose patience is somehow endless and whose hair somehow always looks really good! My literary agent, Cameron McClure of Donald Maass Literary Agency, who snapped this nervous, first-time author up right quick and who always had my back—thank you so much! A lotta love to my feminist mentors at SUNY Oswego and SUNY Brockport and my first feminist inspiration, Dr. Wilma J. Pyle. (I hope you'd be proud, Aunt Wilma!) A huge thanks to my parents, Kathleen and Donald Rich, who encouraged me to use my (always very loud, thanks) voice and who gave me my earliest memories of organizing—stuffing folders for their union meetings around the dining room table. Lastly, but most importantly, thank you to the girls and young activists leading revolutions big and small all over the world. I see you, I'm listening, and I'm ready to follow *your* lead into the future!